THE WORKS 3

Paul Cookson

Paul has been writing and editing books since he was eighteen and is one of the busiest poets you are likely to encounter. Always in demand with his performances and workshops, he has edited over twenty collections in the last seven years. And he's still only in his forties – which is young for a poet. And he's still alive – which is a bigger bonus.

Paul lives in Retford with his wife, Sally, and two children, Sam and Daisy.

A lifelong Everton and Slade fan, Paul has just released a collection of football poems called *Give Us a Goal!*

A Poet A Week

Chosen by
Paul Cookson

MACMILLAN CHILDREN'S BOOKS

*It may be my name on the front of this book,
but I would like to dedicate it to Gaby Morgan.*

*Her eye for the balance of new and old and her pursuit of quality
have been a constant source of inspiration and support. Thanks!*

First published 2004 by Macmillan Children's Books
a division of Macmillan Publishers Limited
20 New Wharf Road, London N1 9RR
Basingstoke and Oxford
www.panmacmillan.com

Associated companies throughout the world

ISBN 0 330 41578 6

A CIP catalogue record for this book is available from the British Library.

Typeset by SX Composing DTP, Rayleigh, Essex
Printed and bound in Great Britain by Mackays of Chatham plc, Kent

Contents

Contents

Contents

Spike Milligan

Jackie Kay

Stewart Henderson

Contents

Christina Rossetti

Vernon Scannell

Gerard Manley Hopkins

Contents

Paul Cookson

Robert Burns

Brian Moses

Contents

Jenny Joseph

Grace Nichols

Carol Ann Duffy

Contents

Peter Dixon

Lewis Carroll

James Berry

Contents

John Clare

James Carter

Clare Bevan

Contents

William Shakespeare

Nick Toczek

Gareth Owen

Contents

David Harmer

Valerie Bloom

William Wordsworth

Contents

John Rice

Eleanor Farjeon

Roger McGough

Contents

Alfred, Lord Tennyson

Andrew Fusek Peters

Gervase Phinn

Contents

Emily Dickinson

Robert Louis Stevenson

Roger Stevens

Contents

Lindsey MacRae

Jan Dean

Pie Corbett

Contents

Wes Magee

Richard Edwards

John Agard

Contents

Edward Thomas

Sue Cowling

Ogden Nash

Contents

Wilfred Owen

Gina Douthwaite

Colin West

Contents

John Hegley

The Works 3 – Introduction

Hello and welcome to *The Works 3*!

It's really exciting to see all these poets together in one collection. I wanted to create a book that would showcase poets and demonstrate the range of their work. So often we see poems in isolation, dotted about in anthologies, but with this collection we get to see seven in a row and we get a better impression of the person behind the poems – the variety of style, tone, voice, rhythm and rhyme. These seven poems give us an insight into the poet and his or her work as a whole.

It's been difficult to find the right seven poems – there were poems I loved but which have appeared in lots of collections and are terribly well-known, so I left them out so that I could include new poems to give the reader something fresh to discover. In many cases I could very easily have chosen many more than seven . . . So here it is – a poet for every single week of the year – one poem a day for a year from some of the very best classic and contemporary poets. Some of the poets are no longer with us, while others continue to explore the very frontiers of poetry in the twenty-first century. One thing I can guarantee is this – no one will leave this book unsatisfied. There is something for everyone in *The Works 3*, and I expect that most poems will be enjoyed by most readers at some time, whether now or later.

One final thought – one of the perks of being an editor is

that you not only get to choose some of your favourite poems by some of your favourite poets, but that you also get to include some of your own poems too. I consider it an honour and a privilege to have my work alongside all the other names in this book.

Enjoy!

Paul Cookson
February 2004.

Steve Turner

At around the age of sixteen Steve Turner began writing poetry in emulation of his best friend, Ginger, who in turn was emulating the songwriter Bob Dylan. Two years later Steve gave his first poetry reading, in the back room of a pub in Northampton, and he has never stopped writing poetry and giving readings.

At the age of twenty-one he came to London and began working as a music journalist, interviewing many of the big pop stars of the day including John Lennon, David Bowie, Marc Bolan and Elton John. His first poetry book was published in 1975 and this was followed by three more poetry books for adults. He began writing poetry for children in the 1990s. His first collection, *The Day I Fell Down the Toilet*, has now sold over 100,000 copies, and has been followed by *Dad, You're Not Funny, The Moon Has Got His Pants On* and *I Was Only Asking*.

Steve Turner

Wait

These are
the good
old days.

Just wait
and see.

I Am on the Kids' Side

I am on the kids' side
in the war against adults.
I don't want to stand still.
I don't want to sit still.
I don't want to be quiet.
I believe that strangers
are for staring at,
bags are for looking into,
paper is for scribbling on.
I want to know Why.
I want to know How.
I wonder What If.
I am on the kids' side
in the war against tedium.
I'm for going home

when stores get packed.
I'm for sleeping in
when parties get dull.
I'm for kicking stones
when conversation sags.
I'm for making noises.
I'm for playing jokes –
especially in life's
more Serious Bits.
I am on the kids' side.
See my sneaky grin,
watch me dance, see me run.
Spit on the carpet, rub it in,
pick my nose in public,
play rock stars in the mirror.
I am on the kids' side.
I want to know why we're not moving.
I'm fed up. I want to go out.
What's that? Can I have one?
It isn't fair. Who's that man?
It wasn't me, I was pushed.
When are we going to go?
I am on the kids' side
putting fun back into words.
Ink pink pen and ink
you go out because you stink.
Stephen Turner is a burner,
urner, murner, purner.
Stephen, weven, peven,
reven, teven, Turnip Top.

I am on the kids' side
in the war against apathy.
Mum, I want to do something.
It must be my turn next.
When can we go out?
I am on the kids' side
and when I grow up,
I want to be a boy.

I Don't Like Girls

I don't like girls. Not me.
Girls are wet.
Girls play girls' games.
I want to go out
with the boys.
Snogging's daft.
I saw it on telly.
I'll never snog a girl.
Not me.

I like some girls.
Some girls are fun.
Some girls are like boys.
They play good games.
You can have a girl
who is your friend,
but that doesn't mean
that she's your *girlfriend*.
Girlfriends are silly.

I quite like girls.
They make me feel funny inside.
It's a nice sort of funny, though.
I dreamed about a girl once.
I don't think girls
really like boys.
Girls only play with girls.

I really like girls.
Girls are great.
They wear skirts.
Snogging's fantastic.
You can play games
that make you feel
funny inside.
I think girls really like me.

I like this girl.
She's great.
When I'm with her
the world falls away.
We think the same thoughts.
We want to be with each other
to the end of the world.

I don't like girls. Not me.
Girls are wet.
They wear skirts.
Girls talk girls' talk.
I want to go out with the lads.
Romance is daft.
They see it all on telly.
You'll never catch me
going all soft.
Not me.

Short Poem

Short poems
are fun.
You can see
at a glance
whether you
like them
or not.

I Like Words

I like words.
Do you like words?
Words aren't hard to find:
Words on walls and words in books,
Words deep in your mind.

Words in jokes
That make you laugh,
Words that seem to smell.
Words that end up inside out,
Words you cannot spell.

Words that fly
And words that crawl,
Words that screech and bump.
Words that glide and words that swing,
Words that bounce and jump.

Words that paint
And words that draw,
Words that make you grin.
Words that make you shake and sweat,
Words that touch your skin.

Words of love
That keep you warm,
Words that make you glad.
Words that hit you, words that hurt,
Words that make you sad.

Words in French
And words in slang,
Words like 'guy' and 'dude'.
Words you make up, words you steal,
Words they say are rude.

I like words.
Do you like words?
Words come out and play.
Words are free and words are friends,
Words are great to say.

Words I Like

Billowing, seaboard, ocean, pearl,
Estuary, shale, maroon;
Harlequin, runnel, ripple, swirl,
Labyrinth, lash, lagoon.

Razorbill, cygnet, songbird, kite,
Cormorant, crag, ravine;
Flickering, sun-burst, dappled, flight,
Fiery, dew, serene.

Asteroid, nova, stardust, moon,
Galaxy, zone, eclipse;
Dynamo, pulsar, planet, rune,
Satellite, spangle, lips.

Boulevard, freeway, turnpike, cruise,
Chevrolet, fin, pavanne;
Tomahawk, firecrest, fantail, fuse,
Saskatchewan, Sioux, Cheyenne.

Tenderness, sweetheart, cherish, miss,
Paramour, fond, befriend;
Affection, cosy, cuddle, kiss,
Family, love, the end.

Sun

Lightbringer
Joymaker
Nightchaser
Cloudshaker.

Foodgrower
Gloomfighter
Heatgiver
Moonlighter.

Sleepender
Icebreaker
Leafrouser
Plantwaker.

Skinbrowner
Nosepeeler
Feetwarmer
Hearthealer.

Edward Lear

Edward Lear was born in London in 1812. He was the twentieth child of a businessman. He was brought up mainly by his older sister, Ann, and earned a living doing drawings of animals and plants. He became a full-time poet later in life when the Earl of Derby gave him some money. He travelled all over the world writing and drawing, but he suffered from illness and depression. He is known for writing nonsense poems, such as 'The Jumblies' and 'The Owl and the Pussy-Cat'. He died in 1888.

There Was an Old Man with a Beard

There was an Old Man with a beard,
Who said, 'It is just as I feared! –
Two Owls and a Hen,
Four Larks and a Wren,
Have all built their nests in my beard!'

Tuesday

There Was an Old Man of Dumbree

There was an Old Man of Dumbree,
Who taught little Owls to drink Tea;
For he said, 'To eat mice
Is not proper or nice,'
That amiable Man of Dumbree.

The Jumblies

They went to sea in a Sieve, they did,
  In a Sieve they went to sea:
In spite of all their friends could say,
On a winter's morn, on a stormy day,
  In a Sieve they went to sea!
And when the Sieve turned round and round,
And every one cried, 'You'll all be drowned!'
They called aloud, 'Our Sieve ain't big,
But we don't care a button! we don't care a fig!
  In a Sieve we'll go to sea!'
    Far and few, far and few,
      Are the lands where the Jumblies live;
      Their heads are green, and their hands are blue,
      And they went to sea in a Sieve.

They sailed away in a Sieve, they did,
　　In a Sieve they sailed so fast,
With only a beautiful pea-green veil
Tied with a riband by way of a sail,
　　To a small tobacco-pipe mast;
And every one said, who saw them go,
'O won't they be soon upset, you know!
For the sky is dark, and the voyage is long,
And happen what may, it's extremely wrong
　　In a Sieve to sail so fast!'
　　　　Far and few, far and few,
　　　　　Are the lands where the Jumblies live;
　　　　Their heads are green, and their hands are blue,
　　　　　And they went to sea in a Sieve.

The water it soon came in, it did,
　　The water it soon came in;
So to keep them dry, they wrapped their feet
In a pinky paper all folded neat,
　　And they fastened it down with a pin.
And they passed the night in a crockery-jar,
And each of them said, 'How wise we are!
Though the sky be dark, and the voyage be long,
Yet we never can think we were rash or wrong,
　　While round in our Sieve we spin!'
　　　　Far and few, far and few,
　　　　　Are the lands where the Jumblies live;
　　　　Their heads are green, and their hands are blue,
　　　　　And they went to sea in a Sieve.

And all night long they sailed away;
    And when the sun went down,
They whistled and warbled a moony song
To the echoing sound of a coppery gong,
    In the shade of the mountains brown.
'O Timballo! How happy we are,
When we live in a sieve and a crockery-jar,
And all night long in the moonlight pale,
We sail away with a pea-green sail,
    In the shade of the mountains brown!'
        Far and few, far and few,
            Are the lands where the Jumblies live;
        Their heads are green, and their hands are blue,
            And they went to sea in a Sieve.

They sailed to the Western Sea, they did,
    To a land all covered with trees,
And they bought an Owl, and a useful Cart,
And a pound of Rice, and a Cranberry Tart,
    And a hive of silvery Bees.
And they bought a Pig, and some green Jack-daws,
And a lovely Monkey with lollipop paws,
And forty bottles of Ring-Bo-Ree,
    And no end of Stilton Cheese.
        Far and few, far and few,
            Are the lands where the Jumblies live;
        Their heads are green, and their hands are blue,
            And they went to sea in a Sieve.

And in twenty years they all came back,
    In twenty years or more,
And every one said, 'How tall they've grown!
For they've been to the Lakes, and the Torrible Zone,
    And the hills of the Chankly Bore;'
And they drank their health, and gave them a feast
Of dumplings made of beautiful yeast;
And every one said, 'If we only live,
We too will go to sea in a Sieve, –
    To the hills of the Chankly Bore!'
        Far and few, far and few,
            Are the lands where the Jumblies live;
        Their heads are green, and their hands are blue,
            And they went to sea in a Sieve.

Thursday

There Was a Young Lady
of Niger

There was a young lady of Niger,
Who smiled as she rode on a tiger;
They came back from the ride
With the lady inside,
And a smile on the face of the tiger.

The Owl and the Pussy-Cat

The Owl and the Pussy-cat went to sea
   In a beautiful pea-green boat,
They took some honey, and plenty of money,
   Wrapped up in a five-pound note.
The Owl looked up to the stars above,
   And sang to a small guitar,
'O lovely Pussy! O Pussy, my love,
      What a beautiful Pussy you are,
         You are,
         You are!
      What a beautiful Pussy you are!'

Pussy said to the Owl, 'You elegant fowl!
   How charmingly sweet you sing!
O let us be married! too long we have tarried:
   But what shall we do for a ring?'
They sailed away, for a year and a day,
   To the land where the Bong-tree grows
And there in a wood a Piggy-wig stood
   With a ring at the end of his nose,
         His nose,
         His nose,
   With a ring at the end of his nose.

17

'Dear Pig, are you willing to sell for one shilling
  Your ring?' Said the Piggy, 'I will.'
So they took it away, and were married next day
  By the Turkey who lives on the hill.
They dined on mince, and slices of quince,
  Which they ate with a runcible spoon;
And hand in hand, on the edge of the sand,
  They danced by the light of the moon,
      The moon,
      The moon,
  They danced by the light of the moon.

Saturday

Calico Pie

Calico Pie,
  The little Birds fly
Down to the calico tree,
  Their wings were blue,
  And they sang 'Tilly-loo!'
Till away they flew, –
    And they never came back to me!
      They never came back!
      They never came back!
    They never came back to me!

Calico Jam,
The little Fish swam,
Over the syllabub sea,
He took off his hat,
To the Sole and the Sprat,
And the Willeby-wat, –
But he never came back to me!
He never came back!
He never came back!
He never came back to me!

Calico Ban,
The little Mice ran,
To be ready in time for tea,
Flippity flup,
They drank it all up,
And danced in the cup, –
But they never came back to me!
They never came back!
They never came back!
They never came back to me!

Calico Drum,
The Grasshoppers come,
The Butterfly, Beetle, and Bee,
Over the ground,
Around and round,
With a hop and a bound, –
But they never came back!
They never came back!
They never came back!
They never came back to me!

Sunday

The Old Person of Ware

There was an Old Person of Ware,
Who rode on the back of a bear:
When they ask'd, 'Does it trot?'
He said, 'Certainly not!
He's a Moppsikon Floppsikon bear!'

Brian Patten

Brian Patten was born in 1946. His collections of poetry include *Love Poems and Armada*. He is famous for his humorous verse for children with books such as *Gargling With Jelly* and *Juggling With Gerbils*. Brian is the author of the award-winning novel, *Mr Moon's Last Case*, and he has edited many anthologies. His latest book is *The Story Giant*, about a man who lives on Dartmoor who has collected every single story known to humankind, except for one . . .

Geography Lesson

Our teacher told us one day he would leave
And sail across a warm blue sea
To places he had only known from maps,
And all his life had longed to be.

The house he lived in was narrow and grey
But in his mind's eye he could see
Sweet-scented jasmine clinging to the walls,
And green leaves burning on an orange tree.

He spoke of the lands he longed to visit,
Where it was never drab or cold.
I couldn't understand why he never left,
And shook off the school's stranglehold.

Then halfway through his final term
He took ill and never returned.
He never got to that place on the map
Where the green leaves of the orange trees burned.

The maps were redrawn on the classroom wall;
His name forgotten, he faded away.
But a lesson he never knew he taught
Is with me to this day.

I travel to where the green leaves burn,
To where the ocean's glass-clear and blue,
To places our teacher taught me to love –
And which he never knew.

Rabbit's Spring

Snow
goes,

Ice
thaws,

Warm
paws!

Brian Patten

The Day I Got My Finger
Stuck Up My Nose

When I got my finger stuck up my nose
I went to a doctor, who said,
'Nothing like this has happened before,
We will have to chop off your head.'

'It's only my finger stuck up my nose,
It's only my finger!' I said.
'I can see what it is,' the doctor replied,
'But we'll still have to chop off your head.'

He went to the cabinet. He took out an axe.
I watched with considerable dread.
'But it's only my finger stuck up my nose.
It's only a finger!' I said.

'Perhaps we can yank it out with a hook
Tied to some surgical thread.
Maybe we can try that,' he replied,
'Rather than chop off your head.'

'I'm never going to pick it again.
I've now learned my lesson,' I said.
'I won't stick my finger up my nose –
I'll stick it in my ear instead.'

Looking for Dad

Whenever Mum and Dad
were full of gloom
they always yelled,
'TIDY UP YOUR ROOM!'
Just because my comics were
scattered here and
everywhere and
because I did not care
where I left my underwear
they yelled, 'You can't watch
TV today
If you don't tidy
All your things away!'
Then one day they
could not care less
about the room's
awful mess.
They seemed more intent
on a domestic argument.
They both looked glum
and instead of me Dad
screeched at Mum.
One night when I
went to bed he
simply vanished.
(Ten past seven, tenth of June.)
I had not tidied
up my room because

I too was
full of gloom.
That night I dreamt
Dad was hidden
beneath the things
I'd been given.
In my dream
I was in despair
and flung about
my underwear
but could not find
him anywhere.
I looked for him
lots and lots
beneath crumpled sheets
and old robots.
I looked in cupboards
and in shoes.
I looked up all
the chimney flues.
I remembered how
he'd seemed to be
unhappier than
even me. When I woke I knew
it was not my room
that filled Mum and Dad
with so much gloom.
Now I stare at all
my old toy cars
and carpets stained

with old Mars bars
and hope he will
come back soon
and admire my very tidy room.
(It is now the twenty-ninth of June.)

Friday

Squeezes

We love to squeeze bananas,
We love to squeeze ripe plums,
And when they are feeling sad
We love to squeeze our mums.

Brian Patten

Gust Becos I Cud Not Spel

Gust becos I cud not spel
It did not mean I was daft
When the boys in school red my riting
Some of them laffed

But now I am the dictater
They have to rite like me
Utherwise they cannot pas
Ther GCSE

Some of the girls wer ok
But those who laffed a lot
Have al bean rownded up
And hav recintly bean shot

The teecher who corected my speling
As not been shot at al
But four the last fifteen howers
As bean standing up against a wal

He has to stand ther until he can spel
Figgymisgrugifooniyn the rite way
I think he will stand ther forever
I just inventid it today

A Small Dragon

I've found a small dragon in the woodshed.
Think it must have come from deep inside a forest
because it's damp and green and leaves
are still reflecting in its eyes.

I fed it on many things, tried grass,
the roots of stars, hazel-nut and dandelion,
but it stared up at me as if to say, I need
foods you can't provide.

It made a nest among the coal,
not unlike a bird's but larger,
it is out of place here
and is quite silent.

If you believed in it I would come
hurrying to your house to let you share my wonder,
but I want instead to see
if you yourself will pass this way.

Ian McMillan

Barnsley FC poet-in-residence and Beat Poet for Humberside Police (the World's first poet-in-residence with a police force), Ian McMillan has been a poet, broadcaster, commentator and programme maker since 1981. He has explored language and communication with schoolchildren, students, teachers, education policy makers, politicians, public services and corporate businesses, in every conceivable location, from an archaeological dig to a Swiss mountain railway.

His performance work has included thousands of gigs since the mid-seventies. Ian started out in folk clubs, performing under the name of Oscar the Frog, singing 'Chattanooga Choo-Choo' while eating a packet of plain crisps, and not swallowing. He performed with Circus of Poets for ten years, and for three years with his long-standing collaborator, the late Martyn Wiley, as Yakety Yak.

Ian currently hosts a weekly show, *The Verb*, on BBC Radio 3, dedicated to investigating spoken words around the globe.

Ian was born in 1956 and lives on the edge of Barnsley with his wife, Catherine, whom he met when he was fourteen, and his three children.

Counting the Stars

It's late at night
and John is counting the stars.

He's walking through the woods
and counting the stars.

The night is clear
and the stars are like salt

on a black tablecloth.
John counts silently,

his lips moving, his head tilted.
It's late at night

and John is counting the stars
until he walks into a tree

that he never saw
because he was counting the stars.

Look at John
lying in the woods.

The woodland creatures are gathering around him
laughing

in little woodland voices.

Moral:
Even when you're looking up,
Don't forget to look down.

Tuesday

Ready Salted

Nothing else happened
that day.

Nothing much, anyway.

I got up, went to school,
did the usual stuff.

Came home, watched telly,
did the usual stuff.

Nothing else happened
that day,

nothing much, anyway,

but the eyeball in the crisps
was enough.

Ten Things Found in a Shipwrecked Sailor's Pocket

A litre of sea.
An unhappy jellyfish.
A small piece of a lifeboat.
A pencil wrapped around with seaweed.
A soaking feather.
The first page of a book called *Swimming is Easy*.
A folded chart showing dangerous rocks.
A photograph of a little girl in a red dress.
A gold coin.
A letter from a mermaid.

Routes

1 The Walk to School

Down Barking-dog Lane
past the street with the boat
   Clouds rush by
   Sometimes it rains

Up Old-lady-waving Road
past the field with the car
   Clouds hang still
   Aeroplanes drone

Down Skateboard Steps
past the shop with the cat
   Clouds make shapes
   Reflect in windowpanes

2. The Drive to School

radio shouts
Mum shouts
belt tight
window steam
Dad shouts
radio shouts
feel hot
feel sick
radio, Mum,
Dad shout
shout shout
every day
same shout
same hot
same sick
same same
same same

Robinson Crusoe's Wise Sayings

You can never have too many turtles' eggs.
I'm the most interesting person in this room.
A beard is as long as I want it to be.

The swimmer on his own doesn't need trunks.
A tree is a good clock.
If you talk to a stone long enough you'll fall asleep.

I know it's Christmas because I cry.
Waving at ships is useless.
Footprints make me happy, unless they're my own.

The Music I Like

The Music I like
Is very special music.

At this moment,
For instance,

I'm listening to the washing machine
Slowing down,

As the gerbil rattles
In its cage,

And my wife runs
Up the stairs

And my next-door neighbour
Cuts his grass.

Music, very special music
Just listen . . .

Sunday

Ten One-Line Poems
about Sport

Golf
That white moon in the blue sky, orbiting.

Cricket
Long late-afternoon shadows as the bowler runs.

Basketball
The clock runs down slower than the players.

Swimmers
Moment of stillness before the start: water-mirror.

Snooker
The giant's necklace broke and the beads fell on to the grass.

Football
This net's for catching slippery goalfish!

Marathon
Last metre: the best and the worst.

Rugby
Flying Easter egg under the H

High Jump
The air holds me like a hand, then lets me go.

Cycling
Here come the fastest paper boys and girls in the world!

John Foster

John Foster was born in 1941 and grew up in a village called Scotby, near Carlisle. He was keen on sports and spent his childhood playing cricket and tennis, and watching Carlisle United football team. He also enjoyed reading. His favourite book was *The Dragon Book of Verse*.

After university, he became an English teacher and taught for twenty years before becoming a full-time writer. While he was teaching, he wrote school textbooks and in 1979 compiled his first poetry anthology. He has now had over one hundred poetry anthologies published and eleven books of his own poetry. The most popular anthology is *Twinkle, Twinkle Chocolate Bar*, and the most popular collection of his own poems is *Four O'Clock Friday*.

He writes poems because he loves words – his favourite word is hullabaloo – and in poems you can play with words. He enjoys entertaining children, but he also wants them to think about serious things, so there are poems about bullying, family break-ups and the environment.

He gets a lot of his ideas from things that have happened to him, like when he broke a window, and when he gave his teddy bear a haircut. Other poems are based on either observation or imagination.

He now lives in a village called Standlake, in Oxfordshire. He is married with two grown-up sons and two grandchildren, Evie and Louis. His wife is called Chris, and when he gets completely stuck while he's drafting a poem, he sometimes shows her what he's doing and she helps him to find a solution.

Summer Storm

Light travels, said Miss,
Faster than sound.
Next time there's a storm,
When you see the lightning,
Start counting slowly in seconds.
If you divide
The number of seconds by three,
It will tell you
How many kilometres you are
From the centre of the storm.

Two nights later
I was woken
By the lashing rain,
The lightning
And the thunder's crash.

I lay,
Huddled beneath the sheet,
As the rain poured down
And lightning lit up the bedroom,
Slowly counting the seconds,
Listening for the thunder
And calculating the distance
As the storm closed in –

Until,
With a blinding flash
And a simultaneous ear-splitting crash,
The storm passed
Directly overhead.

And I shook with fright
As the storm passed on,
Leaving the branches shuddering
And the leaves weeping.

Tuesday

November

November is a grey road
Cloaked in mist.
A twist of wood-smoke
In the gathering gloom.
A scurrying squirrel
Hoarding acorns.
A steel-grey river
Glinting in the twilight.
A grey rope
Knotted around a threadbare tree.

'It isn't right to fight'

You said, 'It isn't right to fight,'
But when we watched the news tonight,
You shook your fist and said
You wished the tyrant and his cronies dead.
When I asked why,
If it's not right to fight,
You gave a sigh.
You shook your head
And sadly said,
'Sometimes a cause is just
And, if there is no other way,
Perhaps, you must.'

Four O'Clock Friday

Four o'clock Friday, I'm home at last,
Time to forget the week that's past.
On Monday, in break they stole my ball
And threw it over the playground wall.
On Tuesday afternoon, in games
They threw mud at me and called me names.
On Wednesday, they trampled my books on the floor,
So Miss kept me in because I swore.
On Thursday, they laughed after the test
'Cause my marks were lower than the rest.
Four o'clock Friday, at last I'm free,
For two whole days they can't get at me.

Dad's Hiding in the Shed

Dad's hiding in the shed.
He's made me swear
Not to tell Mum
That he's hiding in there.

She was having a lie-down
With the curtains drawn.
We were playing cricket
Out on the lawn.

The scores were level.
It was really tense.
Dad had just hit a six
Right over the fence.

I bowled the next ball
As fast as I could.
Dad tried it again
As I knew he would.

But he missed and the ball
Struck him hard on the toe.
He cried out in pain
And, as he did so,

He let go of the bat.
It flew up in an arc
And crashed through the window
Where Mum lay in the dark.

Dad's hiding in the shed.
He's made me swear
Not to tell Mum
That he's hiding in there.

Spells

I crackle and spit. I lick and leap higher.
This is the spell of the raging fire.

I clasp and I grasp. I grip in a vice.
This is the spell of torturing ice.

I claw and I scratch. I screech and I wail.
This is the spell of the howling gale.

I clash and I crash. I rip asunder.
This is the spell of booming thunder.

I whisper. I stroke. I tickle the trees.
This is the spell of the evening breeze.

I slither. I slide. I drift and I dream.
This is the spell of the murmuring stream.

Spring Snow

Snowflakes
Slip from the sky
Like soft white butterflies,
Brush the trees with their flimsy wings,
Vanish.

William Blake

William Blake lived in London. He illustrated his own poems and printed them himself. He rebelled against authority and had many new and exciting visions of how the world could be. He is most famous for the books of poetry *Songs of Innocence* (1789) and *Songs of Experience* (1794). These books revealed two opposite worlds: one in which God is trusted implicitly and there is no question of moral issues; and one in which the fallen state and religious hypocrisy are examined.

The Tyger

Tyger! Tyger! burning bright
In the forests of the night,
What immortal hand or eye
Could frame thy fearful symmetry?

In what distant deeps or skies
Burnt the fire of thine eyes?
On what wings dare he aspire?
What the hand dare seize the fire?

And what shoulder, and what art,
Could twist the sinews of thy heart?
And when thy heart began to beat,
What dread hand? and what dread feet?

What the hammer? what the chain?
In what furnace was thy brain?
What the anvil? what dread grasp
Dare its deadly terrors clasp?

When the stars threw down their spears,
And water'd heaven with their tears,
Did he smile his work to see?
Did he who made the Lamb make thee?

Tyger! Tyger! burning bright
In the forests of the night,
What immortal hand or eye
Dare frame thy fearful symmetry?

And Did Those Feet in Ancient Time

And did those feet in ancient time
Walk upon England's mountains green?
And was the holy lamb of God
On England's pleasant pastures seen?

And did the countenance divine
Shine forth upon our clouded hills?
And was Jerusalem builded here
Among those dark satanic mills?

Bring me my bow of burning gold:
Bring me my arrows of desire:
Bring me my spear: O clouds unfold!
Bring me my chariot of fire.

I will not cease from mental fight,
Nor shall my sword sleep in my hand
Till we have built Jerusalem
In England's green and pleasant land.

A Cradle Song

Sleep Sleep beauty bright
Dreaming oer the joys of night
Sleep Sleep: in thy sleep
Little sorrows sit & weep

Sweet Babe in thy face
Soft desires I can trace
Secret joys & secret smiles
Little pretty infant wiles

As thy softest limbs I feel
Smiles as of the morning steal
Oer thy cheek & oer thy breast
Where thy little heart does rest

O the cunning wiles that creep
In thy little heart asleep
When thy little heart does wake
Then the dreadful lightnings break

From thy cheek & from thy eye
Oer the youthful harvests nigh
Infant wiles & infant smiles
Heaven & Earth of peace beguiles

Thursday

'Great Things are done when men & mountains meet'

Great things are done when Men & Mountains meet
This is not Done by Jostling in the Street

The Lamb

Little Lamb, who made thee?
  Dost thou know who made thee?
Gave thee life, and bid thee feed
By the stream and o'er the mead;
Gave thee clothing of delight,
Softest clothing, woolly, bright;
Gave thee such a tender voice,
Making all the vales rejoice?
  Little Lamb, who made thee?
  Dost thou know who made thee?

Little Lamb, I'll tell thee,
  Little Lamb, I'll tell thee:
He is callèd by thy name,
For He calls himself a Lamb.
He is meek, and He is mild;
He became a little child.
I, a child, and thou a lamb,
We are callèd by His name.
  Little Lamb, God bless thee!
  Little Lamb, God bless thee!

William Blake

The Piper

Piping down the valleys wild,
Piping songs of pleasant glee,
On a cloud I saw a child,
And he laughing said to me:

'Pipe a song about a lamb!'
So I piped with merry cheer.
'Piper, pipe that song again;'
So I piped: he wept to hear.

'Drop thy pipe, thy happy pipe;
Sing thy songs of happy cheer.'
So I sung the same again,
While he wept with joy to hear.

'Piper, sit thee down and write
In a book that all may read.'
So he vanished from my sight,
And I plucked a hollow reed.

And I made a rural pen,
And I stained the water clear,
And I wrote my happy songs
Every child may joy to hear.

from 'Auguries of Innocence'

To see a World in a Grain of Sand
And a Heaven in a Wild Flower,
Hold Infinity in the palm of your hand
And Eternity in an hour.

Spike Milligan

Spike Milligan was born in India. He played the trumpet in various jazz bands when he was young. He joined the British Army at the outbreak of the Second World War, in which he served in the Royal Artillery through the North African and Italian campaigns. In the 1950s he joined Peter Sellers, Harry Secombe, and sometimes Michael Bentine, to make the ground-breaking radio comedy *The Goon Show*. He continued to make more legendary and ground-breaking television programmes, appear in films, and write novels, memoirs and poetry. He was famous for, and loved for, his zany and offbeat sense of humour – and many of his poems, such as 'On the Ning Nang Nong', reflect this.

Onamatapia

Onamatapia!
Thud-Wallop-**CRASH!**
Onamatapia!
Snip-Snap-**GNASH!**
Onamatapia!
Wack-thud-**BASH!**
Onamatapia!
Bong-Ting-**SPLASH!**

Melbourne–Tasmania
April 1980

Tuesday

On the Ning Nang Nong

On the Ning Nang Nong
Where the Cows go Bong!
And the Monkeys all say Boo!
There's a Nong Nang Ning
Where the trees go Ping!
And the tea pots Jibber Jabber Joo.

On the Nong Ning Nang
All the mice go Clang!
And you just can't catch 'em when they do!
So it's Ning Nang Nong!
Cows go Bong!
Nong Nang Ning!
Trees go Ping!
Nong Ning Nang!
The mice go Clang!
What a noisy place to belong,
Is the Ning Nang Ning Nang Nong!!

Wednesday

The Land of the Bumbley Boo

In the Land of the Bumbley Boo
The people are red white and blue,
They never blow noses,
Or ever wear closes,
What a sensible thing to do!

In the Land of the Bumbley Boo
You can buy Lemon pie at the Zoo;
They give away Foxes
In little Pink Boxes
And Bottles of Dandylion Stew.

In the Land of the Bumbley Boo
You never see a Gnu,
But thousands of cats
Wearing trousers and hats
Made of Pumpkins and Pelican Glue!

Chorus
Oh, the Bumbley Boo! the Bumbley Boo!
That's the place for me and you!
So hurry! Let's run!
The train leaves at one!
For the Land of the Bumbley Boo!
The wonderful Bumbley Boo-Boo-Boo!
The Wonderful Bumbley BOO!!!

Thursday

Sardines

A baby Sardine
Saw her first submarine:
She was scared and watched through a peephole.

'Oh, come, come, come,'
Said the Sardine's mum,
'It's only a tin full of people.'

Spike Milligan

Bump!

Things that go 'bump!' in the night,
Should not really give one a fright.
It's the hole in each ear
That lets in the fear,
That, and the absence of light!

Saturday

Rain

There are holes in the sky
Where the rain gets in,
But they're ever so small
That's why rain is thin.

Contagion

Elephants are contagious!
Be careful how you tread.
An Elephant that's been trodden on
Should be confined to bed!

Leopards are contagious too.
Be careful tiny tots.
They don't give you a temperature
But lots and lots – of spots.

The Herring is a lucky fish,
From all disease inured.
Should he be ill when caught at sea:
Immediately – he's cured!

Jackie Kay

Jackie Kay was born and brought up in Scotland. She has published three collections of poetry for adults and she has also written three collections of poetry for children – *Two's Company* (which won The Signal Award), *Three Has Gone* and *The Frog Who Dreamed She Was an Opera Singer*, winner of the 1999 Signal Award. Her novel for children, *Strawgirl*, was published by Macmillan Children's Books.

She lives in Manchester with her son. She teaches Creative Writing at Newcastle University and is a fellow of the Royal Society of Literature.

Brendon Gallacher

(for my brother, Maxie)

He was seven and I was six, my Brendon Gallacher.
He was Irish and I was Scottish, my Brendon Gallacher.
His father was in prison; he was a cat burglar.
My father was a communist party full-time worker.
He had six brothers and I had one, my Brendon Gallacher.

He would hold my hand and take me by the river
Where we'd talk all about his family being poor.
He'd get his mum out of Glasgow when he got older.
A wee holiday some place nice. Some place far.
I'd tell my mum about my Brendon Gallacher

How his mum drank and his daddy was a cat burglar.
And she'd say, 'why not have him round to dinner?'
No, no, I'd say, he's got big holes in his trousers.
I like meeting him by the burn in the open air.
Then one day after we'd been friends two years,

One day when it was pouring and I was indoors,
My mum says to me, 'I was talking to Mrs Moir
Who lives next door to your Brendon Gallacher
Didn't you say his address was 24 Novar?
She says there are no Gallachers at 24 Novar

There never have been any Gallachers next door.'
And he died then, my Brendon Gallacher,
Flat out on my bedroom floor, his spiky hair,
His impish grin, his funny flapping ear.
Oh Brendon, Oh my Brendon Gallacher.

Tuesday

The Moon at Knowle Hill

The moon was married last night
and nobody saw
dressed up in her ghostly dress
for the summer ball.

The stars shimmied in the sky
and danced a whirligig;
the moon vowed to be true
and lit up the corn-rigs.

She kissed the dark lips of the sky
Above the summer house
She in her pale white dress
swooned across the vast sky

The moon was married last night
the beautiful belle of the ball
and nobody saw her at all
except a small girl in a navy dress

who witnessed it all.

Summer Romance

I was best friends with Sabah
the whole long summer;
I admired her handwriting,
the way she smiled into
the summer evening,
her voice, melted butter.
The way her chin shone
under a buttercup.
Everyone let Sabah
go first in a long
hot summer queue.
The way she always looked
fancy, the way
she said 'Fandango',
and plucked her banjo;
her big purple bangle
banged at her wrist;

her face lit by the angle
poise lamp in her room,
her hair all a tangle,
damp from the summer heat,
Sabah's eyes sparkled all summer.
But when the summer was gone
and the winter came,
in walked Big Heather Murphy.
Sabah turned her lovely head
towards her. I nearly died.
Summer holidays burn with lies.

Thursday

The World of Trees

(inspired by the Forest of Burnley)

S*ycamore. Mountain Ash. Beech. Birch. Oak.*

In the middle of the forest the trees stood.
And the beech knew the birch was there.
And the mountain ash breathed the same air
as the sycamore, and everywhere

The wind blew, the trees understood each other:
How the river made the old oak lean to the east,
How the felled beech changed the currents of the wind,
How the two common ash formed a canapé,

And grew in a complementary way.
Between them they shared a full head of hair.
Some amber curls of the one could easily
belong to the other: twin trees, so similar.

Sycamore. Mountain Ash. Beech. Birch. Oak.

Some trees crouched in the forest, waiting
for another tree to die so that they could
shoot up suddenly in that new space;
stretch out comfortably for the blue sky.

Some trees grew mysterious mushroom fungi,
shoelace, honey, intricate as a grandmother's lace.
The wind fluttered the leaves; the leaves flapped their wings.
Birds flew from the trees. Sometimes they'd sing.

The tall trees, compassionate, understood everything:
Grief – they stood stock still, branches drooped in despair.
Fear – they exposed their many roots, tugged their gold hair.
Anger – they shook in the storm, pointed their bony fingers.

Sycamore. Mountain Ash. Beech. Birch. Oak.

The trees knew each other's secrets.
In the deep green heart of the forest.
Each tree loved another tree best.
Each tree, happy to rest, leant a little to the east,

Or to the west, when the moon loomed high above,
the big white eye of the woods.
And they stood together as one in the dark,
with the stars sparkling from their branches,

Completely at ease, breathing in the cold night air
swishing a little in the breeze,
dreaming of glossy spring leaves
in the fine, distinguished company of trees.

Sycamore. Mountain Ash. Beech. Birch. Oak.

Friday

Black Ann

They call me Black Ann all the way up the Mississippi.
They call me Black Ann all the way up the Mississippi.
I cook on the Mississippi steamboat, everyone knows me.
I been many big places, but my heart's in Missouri.

When I think of Missouri, I think of my son Billy.
My son Billy in Missouri without his own Mammy.
Is he sleeping at night, no mammy singing sweetly?
He's working for the bossman even tho' he's just a pickney.

At night when the steamboat takes me down the Mississippi,
I get to thinkin' 'bout Billy, all I do is worry.
Tired of cookin', I get too tired to do any sleepin',
It's Billy in the mornin'; it's Billy in the evenin'.

They call me Black Ann all the way up the Mississippi.
Everybody knows my steamboat, praises my cookin' highly.
When I get enough money, I'm buying back my Billy.
The bossman he done told me, he cost a pretty penny.

Five hundred dollars to buy me back my own son Billy.
Well every meal I make is a meal for my sweet Billy.
Every mouthful they take is a mouthful for my boy.
One day I'll buy my Billy way down in that Missouri.

It's been three long years since I set eyes on my Billy.
I'm praying Billy's not forgotten his good old Mammy.
I'm going to be a big surprise one day in Missouri.
I'm going to havta say, 'Billy, son, I'm your own Mammy.'

They call me Black Ann all the way up the Mississippi.

Jackie Kay

The Hole Story

You sure you want the hole story?
All right, you got the hole story.
I was born tiny, mendable
in the smelly sock of Will MacDowall.

Soon, I was the dark sweet cavity
in the slippy mouth of Lisa MacVittie.
But hey, I had high holes for myself.
Fuelled by ambition, I craved big roles.

I was a hole for a mole, a mouse, a man,
a key, a button, a spy, a can.
I lived through holes peeping and weeping,
happy holes, sad holes, big holes, deep in.

You name them; I've been them – Polo
mint. Loads of good parts playing solo.
I've been a hole in a halo, a hole in a doughnut,
I've aimed high and low, meant a whole lot, but

I've been all holes to all people.
Pupil, nostril, earhole, unmentionable!
Had cheesy days in Emmental cheese,
gooey days in honeycombs from bees.

I've picked a hole and made it holy,
the secret lagoon, the tearful valley.
I've played every role a hole can play:
snooker, basketball, golf, got a birdie.

The sudden shock of the hard white ball,
the thrill-swoop of the basketball.
O there was nothing I hadn't seen;
there was no hole I hadn't been.

That was my downhole. I wanted to be bigger and bigger.
Till before I could say *Hallelujah*
I was the black hole then the hole in the earth.
The saddest hole in the whole world is the hole in the
    earth.

I am the abyss. You can't avoid me.
Hear my howl of anguish. Stop me.
I didn't mean to get so out of control.
O to be a wee hole!

O to be a wee hole!
To go back to Will MacDowall's
woolly, grey, smelly sock.
O to turn back the clock.

Jackie Kay

Sassenachs

Me and my best pal (well, she was
till a minute ago) are off to London.
First trip on an intercity alone.
When we got on we were the same
kind of excited – jigging on our seats,
staring at everyone. But then,
I remembered I had to be sophisticated.
So when Jenny started shouting,
'Look at that, the land's flat already,'
when we were just outside Glasgow
(Motherwell actually) I'd feel myself flush.
Or even worse, 'Sassenach country!
Wey Hey Hey.' The tartan tammy
sitting proudly on top of her pony;
the tartan scarf swinging like a tail.
The nose pressed to the window.
'England's not so beautiful, is it?'
And we haven't even crossed the border!
And the train's jazzy beat joins her:
Sassenachs Sassenachs here we come.
Sassenachs Sassenachs Rum Tum Tum
Sassenachs Sassenachs How do you do.
Sassenachs Sassenachs WE'LL GET YOU.

Then she loses momentum, so out come
the egg mayonnaise sandwiches and
the big bottle of Bru. 'My ma's done us proud,'
says Jenny, digging in, munching loud.
The whole train is an egg and I'm inside it.
I try to remain calm; Jenny starts it again,
Sassenachs Sassenachs Rum Tum Tum.

Finally we get there: London, Euston;
and the first person on the platform
gets asked – 'Are you a genuine Sassenach?'
I want to die, but instead I say, '*Jenny!*'
He replies in that English way –
'I beg your pardon,' and Jenny screams
'Did you hear that Voice?'
And we both die laughing, clutching
our stomachs at Euston.

Stewart Henderson

Stewart Henderson was born and brought up in Liverpool, and started writing poetry when he was fourteen. He had some poems published in various poetry magazines that were thriving around that time in Liverpool. Then he started to perform his poetry in various pubs and clubs around Merseyside. All very exciting. But he had a plan. (A poet with plans? How come?) He wanted his poetry to reach a wider public, which meant moving away from Liverpool to London, to see if any one of the major London publishing houses would take his poems. This eventually happened. And before that he started to perform his poetry on various networked BBC radio and television programmes.

As well as his poetry activities, he writes and presents various documentaries for BBC radio, including presenting the weekly interactive programme about knowledge, *Questions, Questions*, for BBC Radio 4. He also writes songs with the completely ace Welsh singer/songerwriter Martyn Joseph. It's great being a poet – try it!

How do you fuss an octopus?

How do you fuss an octopus?
Make it count to nine.
How do you fold an ostrich?
How many is 'a swine' –

Is it singular or plural?
Do hyenas ever cry?
How long ago did starfish
fall from the ocean sky?

How do you cook a cuckoo?
When should you comb a hare?
Is the reason they're magnetic
why they're called a 'polar' bear?

And has a money spider
ever been in debt?
So does a wobbly jellyfish
take much time to set?

Is the skylark always playing
jokes above your head?
Is it possible to really tell
when a flea has fled?

Has the crouching cricket
ever played at Lords?
And watch out if that long-nosed fish
ever crosses swords.

Does a praying mantis
need to go to church?
When fishing should you take a cage
if you're catching perch?

Who stood on the flatfish?
That was really cruel.
All these questions in my head
as I walk home from school.

Tuesday

Sounds

Crunching ginger biscuits
is like hearing soldiers tread
marching over gravel
on the inside of your head.

Chewing a marshmallow
is nowhere near as loud.
It's the smaller, sweet equivalent
of swallowing a cloud.

I'm sorry

I'm sorry that I'm clever.
I'm sorry that I'm bright.
I'm sorry I embarrass you
by choosing not to fight

in the playground after school
with Spig, the bully boy.
I'm sorry that I let you down.
I'm sorry I annoy.

I'm sorry that I'm swotty;
that I don't have a tattoo.
I'm sorry that I made you wince
at next door's barbecue

by quoting bits of Shakespeare,
and not passing on the chance
of finishing the evening
with a little ballet dance.

I'm sorry I'm peculiar,
for staying quiet for hours;
that my idea of happiness
is reading about flowers.

I'm sorry I can't skateboard.
I'm sorry for my size.
I'm sorry I find football
a pointless exercise.

I'm sorry I'm your first born;
that I don't make you glad.
I'm sorry you're not proud of me.
I'm really sorry, Dad.

Thursday

Secret Friend

I have a secret friend
who glistens, swirls and laps,
who's older than the oldest bone,
well travelled, wise, perhaps.

I'll ask her if she knows you,
you're by yourself, like me,
then we could go together
to our secret friend, the Sea.

Who left Grandad at the chip shop?

'Who left
Grandad at the chip shop?
Who poured
syrup down the sink?
Which one
left the freezer open?
Why don't
any of you think?

Why's the
rabbit in the wardrobe?
How did
Marmite get up there?
What's this
melted biro doing?
Don't you know
socks come in a pair?

When's this
filthy games kit needed?
Where's the
barbecue fork gone?' –
Our house
is a haze of questions,
best not
answer every one.

Stewart Henderson

Emily prays to elephants

I know you're out there somewhere
making broad cloud shapes in the dark
I know you're out there
eating good things and
trumpeting at lionesses
as they sneak towards your bare babies
with their bad, padding plans.

That's when I change channels
And watch the adverts.
It's a way of vanishing
because there's nothing I can do.

You are so big in my heart,
so perhaps we could make a pact
and I will cry with you.

What a space you must have to live in.
I see you drifting towards
warm waterholes in the buzzing heat.

I have never bathed in mud
but sometimes when my sister gets out
the bath
I imagine I am with you
and we lie half-submerged
in the chocolate water
listening to a host of flamingos
taking off,
a pink paradise that's always travelling.

It is all rather cramped here.
Squeezed streets with sirens
and ice cream tunes,
while you're out there
not knowing about me being here.

You glowing grey in the blazing haze;
me in the damp dusk
being driven to a swimming lesson
where I will float and pretend
that I am with you.

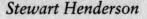

Stewart Henderson

Always making things

I made the splash,
the whirlpool, the surf,
the wonder of thunder,
the sounds of the earth.

I formed the egg,
the armpit, the pear,
the parrot, the carrot,
the goat's glassy stare.

I shaped the twig,
the walrus, the stoat,
the leopard, the shepherd,
the toad's puffing throat.

I breathed the bud,
the iris, the haze,
the tiger, the Eiger,
the ticking of days.

I thought the sprout,
the cactus, the deep,
the blossom, the possum,
the donkey asleep.

I grew the sap,
the desert, the dawn,
the eagle, the beagle,
the mown summer lawn.

I dreamt the wren,
Orion, the kiss,
the moose and the goose and
the cat's arch-backed hiss.

I made the ant,
the vastness, the dew –

But the best of my heart
and the height of my heart
and the light of my heart
was
when I made you.

Christina Rossetti

Christina Rossetti was brought up in London. Her family lived in a whirlwind of literature, religion and politics. Her brother, Dante Gabriel Rossetti, was one of the pre-Raphaelite painters – a very important movement in art in the Victorian period. Christina was often ill and so she wrote a lot of poetry at home. Her poems were mostly romantic or religious, but she occasionally wrote specifically for children. Her work is full of yearning and beautiful sadness, and it often seems that death is not far away. Her most famous poems include 'In the Bleak Mid-Winter' and 'Hurt No Living Thing'.

Seasons

In Springtime when the leaves are young,
Clear dewdrops gleam like jewels, hung
On boughs the fair birds roost among.

When Summer comes with sweet unrest,
Birds weary of their mother's breast,
And look abroad and leave the nest.

In Autumn ere the waters freeze,
The swallows fly across the seas: –
If we could fly away with these!

In Winter when the birds are gone,
The sun himself looks starved and wan,
And starved the snow he shines upon.

Christina Rossetti

A Birthday

My heart is like a singing bird,
  Whose nest is in a watered shoot;
My heart is like an apple-tree
  Whose boughs are bent with thick-set fruit;
My heart is like a rainbow shell
  That paddles in a halcyon sea;
My heart is gladder than all these
  Because my love is come to me.

Raise me a dais of silk and down;
  Hang it with vair and purple dyes;
Carve it in doves and pomegranates,
  And peacocks with a hundred eyes;
Work it in gold and silver grapes,
  In leaves and silver fleurs-de-lys;
Because the birthday of my life
  Is come, my love is come to me.

Remember

Remember me when I am gone away,
   Gone far away into the silent land;
   When you can no more hold me by the hand
Nor I half turn to go yet turning stay.
Remember me when no more day by day
   You tell me of our future that you planned:
   Only remember me; you understand
It will be late to counsel then or pray.
Yet if you should forget me for a while
   And afterwards remember, do not grieve:
   For if the darkness and corruption leave
   A vestige of the thoughts that once I had,
Better by far you should forget and smile
   Than that you should remember and be sad.

The Caterpillar

Brown and furry
Caterpillar in a hurry,
Take your walk
To the shady leaf, or stalk,
Or what not,
Which may be the chosen spot.
No toad to spy you,
Hovering bird of prey pass by you;
Spin and die,
To live again a butterfly.

Hurt No Living Thing

Hurt no living thing,
Ladybird nor butterfly,
Nor moth with dusty wing,
Nor cricket chirping cheerily,
Nor grasshopper, so light of leap,
Nor dancing gnat,
Nor beetle fat,
Nor harmless worms that creep.

What is Pink?

What is pink? A rose is pink
By the fountain's brink.
What is red? A poppy's red
In its barley bed.
What is blue? The sky is blue
Where the clouds float through.
What is white? A swan is white
Sailing in the light.
What is yellow? Pears are yellow,
Rich and ripe and mellow.
What is green? The grass is green,
With small flowers between.
What is violet? Clouds are violet
In the summer twilight.
What is orange? Why, an orange,
Just an orange!

Christina Rossetti

In the Bleak Mid-Winter

In the bleak mid-winter
   Frosty wind made moan,
Earth stood hard as iron,
   Water like a stone;
Snow had fallen, snow on snow,
   Snow on snow,
In the bleak mid-winter
   Long ago.

Our God, Heaven cannot hold Him
   Nor earth sustain;
Heaven and earth shall flee away
   When he comes to reign:
In the bleak mid-winter
   A stable-place sufficed
The Lord God Almighty
   Jesus Christ.

Enough for Him, whom cherubim
   Worship night and day,
A breastful of milk
   And a mangerful of hay;
Enough for Him, whom angels
   Fall down before,
The ox and ass and camel
   Which adore.

Angels and archangels
  May have gathered there,
Cherubim and seraphim
  Thronged the air;
But only His mother
  In her maiden bliss
Worshipped the Beloved
  With a kiss.

What can I give Him,
  Poor as I am?
If I were a shepherd
  I would bring a lamb,
If I were a Wise Man
  I would do my part, –
Yet what I can I give Him,
  Give my heart.

Vernon Scannell

Vernon Scannell was born in 1922. He served in the Gordon Highlanders in the Second World War and was wounded in Normandy. An ex-professional boxer, he is now a novelist, poet and critic. He is married with five children and umpteen grandchildren. Vernon has won the Heinemann Award for Literature, the Cholmondoley Poetry Prize and the Society of Authors' Travelling Scholarship for his poetry. He lives in West Yorkshire on a diet of ice cream and Guinness.

Jelly-lover

Jill likes stuff that wobbles, quivers,
Trembles and gives little shivers,
Ripples, promising rich pleasure,
Glitters like Aladdin's treasure,
Green or red or orange, yellow,
Sharp and fruity, sweet and mellow.
Jill likes jelly in the belly,
She would eat it from a welly;
Loves to see it shake and shudder,
Brightly joggle, jounce and judder.
She adores its slippery motion
And could wallow in an ocean,
Not of green and foamy briny
But lime jelly, smooth and shiny.
Jill, whose best friend calls her Jilly,
Said, 'I hope I don't sound silly
If I say my dream vacation
Has to be an invitation
To an island, gold and shining,
Where I'd spend all day reclining
By a sprinkling sherbet fountain
Shaded by a jelly mountain.'

Vernon Scannell

The Day that Summer Died

From all around the mourners came
  The day that Summer died,
From hill and valley, field and wood
  And lane and mountainside.

They did not come in funeral black
  But every mourner chose
Gorgeous colours or soft shades
  Of russet, yellow, rose.

Horse chestnut, oak and sycamore
  Wore robes of gold and red;
The rowan sported scarlet beads;
  No bitter tears were shed.

Although at dusk the mourners heard,
  As a small wind softly sighed,
A touch of sadness in the air
  The day that Summer died.

Jason's Trial

Jason was a football freak;
    He really loved the game:
To be a first-class footballer
    Was his one aim.

He practised every day and played
    Again each night in dream;
When he was twelve they chose him for
    The school's first team.

He was quite brilliant. Five years passed
    And – though rarely this occurs –
It seemed his dreams might all come true:
    He was given a trial by Spurs.

He played a blinder on the day;
    The spectators cheered and roared,
And after the match he was asked to appear
    Before the Selection Board.

The Chairman said, 'I've got the reports
    From our experts who watched you play:
Your speed and ball-control were fine;
    For tackling you get an A.

And when our striker scored his goal
   You were first to jump on his back
And when *you* scored you punched the air
   Before you resumed the attack.

So far, so good; but you were weak
   On the thing our lads do best;
It seems you hardly spat at all,
   So you failed the spitting-test.

But don't despair. If you go home
   And practise every day
You still might learn to spit with style
   In the true professional way.

Thursday

Epitaph for a Gifted Man

He was not known among his friends for wit;
He owned no wealth, nor did he crave for it.
His looks would never draw a second glance;
He could not play an instrument or dance,
Or sing, or paint, nor would he ever write
The music, plays, or poems that delight
And win the whole world's worship and applause.
He did not fight for any noble cause;
Showed neither great extravagance nor thrift;
But he loved greatly: that was his one gift.

The Apple-Raid

Darkness came early, though not yet cold;
Stars were strung on the telegraph wires;
Street lamps spilled pools of liquid gold;
The breeze was spiced with garden fires.

That smell of burnt leaves, the early dark,
Can still excite me but not as it did
So long ago when we met in the park –
Myself, John Peters and David Kidd.

We moved out of town to the district where
The lucky and wealthy had their homes
With garages, gardens, and apples to spare
Clustered in the trees' green domes.

We chose the place we meant to plunder
And climbed the wall and tip-toed through
The secret dark. Apples crunched under
Our feet as we moved through the grass and dew.

We found the lower boughs of a tree
That were easy to reach. We stored the fruit
In pockets and jerseys until all three
Boys were heavy with their tasty loot.

Safe on the other side of the wall
We moved back to town and munched as we went.
I wonder if David remembers at all
That little adventure, the apples' fresh scent.

Strange to think that he's fifty years old,
That tough little boy with scabs on his knees;
Stranger to think that John Peters lies cold
In an orchard in France beneath apple trees.

Saturday

I Bit an Apple . . .

I bit an apple and the flesh was sweet:
Juice tingled on the tongue and from the fruit
Arose a scent that memory received
And in a flash raised ghosts of apple trees,
Leaves blistered with minutest bulbs of rain
Bewildering an autumn drawing room
Where carpets stained with unaccustomed shadow
Heard one old table creak, perhaps moved too
By some remembrance of a former time
When summer, like a lover, came to him
And laid amazing offerings at his feet.
I bit an apple and the spell was sweet.

My Dog

My dog belongs to no known breed,
    A bit of this and that.
His head looks like a small haystack;
    He's lazy, smelly, fat.

If I say, 'Sit!' he walks away.
    When I throw stick or ball
He flops down in the grass as if
    He had no legs at all.

Then looks at me with eyes that say,
    'You threw the thing, not me.
You want it back? Then get it back.
    Fair's fair, you must agree.'

He is a thief. Last week but one
    He stole the Sunday roast
And showed no guilt at all as we
    Sat down to beans on toast.

The only time I saw him run –
    And he went like a flash –
Was when a mugger in the park
    Tried to steal my cash.

My loyal brave companion flew
　Like a missile to the gate
And didn't stop till safely home.
　He left me to my fate.

And would I swap him for a dog
　Obedient, clean and good,
An honest, faithful, lively chap?
　Oh boy, I would, I would!

Gerard Manley Hopkins

Gerard Manley Hopkins was born in Stratford to Anglican parents and died in Dublin a Jesuit. It was in Oxford that he made his conversion after he met John Newman. Unfortunately, his decision to become a Jesuit meant he burnt his poetry because he now considered it to be against Jesuit principles. Luckily, he came to realize that he had been wrong and started to compose poetry that challenged the conventions of style. In fact, his poems were so radical that they were not published in his lifetime. It was his good friend Robert Bridges, whom he met at Oxford and who became Poet Laureate in 1913, who made sure Hopkins's works were published in 1918. One of his most famous poems is 'Pied Beauty'.

Gerard Manley Hopkins

God's Grandeur

The world is charged with the grandeur of God.
 It will flame out, like shining from shook foil;
 It gathers to a greatness, like the ooze of oil
Crushed. Why do men then now not reck his rod?
Generations have trod, have trod, have trod;
 And all is seared with trade; bleared, smeared with toil;
 And wears man's smudge and shares man's smell: the soil
Is bare now, nor can foot feel, being shod.

And for all this, nature is never spent;
 There lives the dearest freshness deep down things;
And though the last lights off the black West went
 Oh, morning, at the brown brink eastward, springs –
Because the Holy Ghost over the bent
 World broods with warm breast and with ah! bright wings.

Pied Beauty

Glory be to God for dappled things –
   For skies of couple-colour as a brinded cow;
      For rose-moles in all stipple upon trout that swim;
Fresh-firecoal chestnut-falls; finches' wings;
   Landscape plotted and pieced – fold, fallow, and plough;
      And áll trádes, their gear and tackle and trim.
All things counter, original, spare, strange;
   Whatever is fickle, freckled (who knows how?)
      With swift, slow; sweet, sour; adazzle, dim;
He fathers-forth whose beauty is past change:
             Praise him.

Binsey Poplars

felled 1879

My aspens dear, whose airy cages quelled,
Quelled or quenched in leaves the leaping sun,
All felled, felled, are all felled;
  Of a fresh and following folded rank
     Not spared, not one
     That dandled a sandalled
    Shadow that swam or sank
On meadow and river and wind-wandering weed-
    winding bank.

O if we but knew what we do
    When we delve or hew –
  Hack and rack the growing green!
    Since country is so tender
To touch, her being só slender,
That, like this sleek and seeing ball
But a prick will make no eye at all,
Where we, even where we mean

     To mend her we end her,
    When we hew or delve:
After-comers cannot guess the beauty been.
  Ten or twelve, only ten or twelve
    Strokes of havoc únselve
     The sweet especial scene,
    Rural scene, a rural scene,
    Sweet especial rural scene.

Inversnaid

This darksome burn, horseback brown,
His rollrock highroad roaring down,
In coop and in comb the fleece of his foam
Flutes and low to the lake falls home.

A windpuff-bonnet of fáwn-fróth
Turns and twindles over the broth
Of a pool so pitchblack, féll-frówning,
It rounds and rounds Despair to drowning.

Degged with dew, dappled with dew
Are the groins of the braes that the brook treads through,
Wiry heathpacks, flitches of fern,
And the beadbonny ash that sits over the burn.

What would the world be, once bereft
Of wet and of wilderness? Let them be left,
O let them be left, wildness and wet;
Long live the weeds and the wilderness yet.

Heaven-Haven

A nun takes the veil

I have desired to go
　　Where springs not fail,
To fields where flies no sharp and sided hail
　　And a few lilies blow.

And I have asked to be
　　Where no storms come,
Where the green swell is in the havens dumb,
　　And out of the swing of the sea.

Hurrahing in Harvest

Summer ends now; now, barbarous in beauty, the stooks
  rise
    Around; up above, what wind-walks! what lovely
      behaviour
    Of silk-sack clouds! has wilder, wilful-wavier
Meal-drift moulded ever and melted across skies?

I walk, I lift up, I lift up heart, eyes,
    Down all that glory in the heavens to glean our Saviour;
    And, éyes, heárt, what looks, what lips yet gave you a
Rapturous love's greeting of realer, of rounder replies?

And the azurous hung hills are his world-wielding shoulder
    Majestic – as a stallion stalwart, very-violet-sweet! –
These things, these things were here and but the beholder
    Wanting; which two when they once meet,
The heart réars wings bold and bolder
    And hurls for him, O half hurls earth for him off under
      his feet.

Gerard Manley Hopkins

Spring and Fall

to a young child

Márgarét, áre you grieving
Over Goldengrove unleaving?
Leáves líke the things of man, you
With your fresh thoughts care for, can you?
Ah! ás the heart grows older
It will come to such sights colder
By and by, nor spare a sigh
Though worlds of wanwood leafmeal lie;
And yet you will weep and know why.
Now no matter, child, the name:
Sórrow's springs áre the same.
Nor mouth had, no nor mind, expressed
What heart heard of, ghost guessed:
It is the blight man was born for,
It is Margaret you mourn for.

Paul Cookson

Paul Cookson was born in 1961, and was brought up just outside Preston, in Lancashire, where his early ambitions were to play football for Everton, or electric guitar for Slade. His work experience has included chicken catching, selling shoes, market gardening, working with children with special needs, being president of a students' union, interviewing pop stars and writing record and concert reviews. He published his first collection of poems in 1978 and since then has published over fifteen solo collections for adults and children under his own imprint, A Twist in the Tale. He taught full-time for five years, but since 1989 has worked as poet, performing in thousands of schools and venues throughout the country. As well as being a poet Paul is also well known as a superhero, The Amazing Captain Concorde (thanks to a cunning disguise of plastic nose and bright red underpants). If you want, he could come to your school and save you from the dreaded Literacy Hour!

Paul often works with David Harmer in the popular performance poetry duo Spill the Beans, and has appeared on radio and television. He still listens to Slade and supports Everton Football Club. If he has any spare time, he tends to spend too much money on CDs, books, loud shirts, and plays five-a-side football.

Paul Cookson

Full of Surprises

This poem is full of surprises
Each line holds something new
This poem is full of surprises
Especially for you . . .

It's full of tigers roaring
It's full of loud guitars
It's full of comets soaring
It's full of shooting stars

It's full of pirates fighting
It's full of winning goals
It's full of alien sightings
It's full of rock and roll

It's full of rainbows beaming
It's full of eagles flying
It's full of dreamers dreaming
It's full of teardrops drying

It's full of magic spells
It's full of wizards' pointy hats
It's full of fairy elves
It's full of witches and black cats

It's full of dragons breathing fire
It's full of dinosaurs
It's full of mountains reaching higher
It's full of warm applause

It's full of everything you need
It's full of more besides
It's full of food, the world to feed
It's full of fairground rides

It's full of love and happiness
It's full of dreams come true
It's full of things that are the best
Especially for you

It's jammed and crammed and packed and stacked
With things both old and new
This poem is full of surprises
Especially for you.

Paul Cookson

The Haiku Monster

The haiku monster
Gobbles up the syllables
Crunching words and CHOMP!

The haiku monster
slurps the 's' in _paghetti
Bites 'b's for _reakfast

The haiku monster
Jumbles all the telrets pu
Makes   disappear

The haiku monster
Nibbles on the v w ls   nd
Chews consonants u .

The haiku monster,
Alphabet joker, plays with
The lettuce and worms.

The haiku monster
Hides rude words in the poem
And spoils bum snog vest.

Mixes up the lines
The haiku monster
Ruining all the layout.

Coolscorin' Matchwinnin' Celebratin' Striker!

I'm a shirt removin' crowd salutin'
handstandin' happy landin'
rockin' rollin' divin' slidin'
posin' poutin' loud shoutin'
pistol packin' smoke blowin'
flag wavin' kiss throwin'
hipswingin' armwavin'
breakdancin' cool ravin'
shoulder shruggin' team huggin'
hot shootin' rootin' tootin'
somersaultin' fence vaultin'
last-minute goal grinnin'
shimmy shootin' shin spinnin'
celebratin' cup winnin' STRIKER!

Paul Cookson

Let No One Steal Your Dreams

Let no one steal your dreams
Let no one tear apart
The burning of ambition
That fires the drive inside your heart.

Let no one steal your dreams
Let no one tell you that you can't
Let no one hold you back
Let no one tell you that you won't.

Set your sights and keep them fixed
Set your sights on high
Let no one steal your dreams
Your only limit is the sky.

Let no one steal your dreams
Follow your heart
Follow your soul
For only when you follow them
Will you feel truly whole.

Set your sights and keep them fixed
Set your sights on high
Let no one steal your dreams
Your only limit is the sky.

Father's Hands

Father's hands
large like frying pans
broad as shovel blades
strong as weathered spades.

Father's hands
finger ends ingrained with dirt
permanently stained from work
ignoring pain and scorning hurt.

I once saw him walk boldly up to a swan
that had landed in next door's drive and wouldn't move.
The police were there because swans are a protected species,
but didn't do anything, but my dad walked up to it,
picked it up and carried it away. No problem.
Those massive wings that can break a man's bones
were held tight, tight by my father's hands
and I was proud of him that day, really proud.

Father's hands
tough as leather on old boots
firmly grasping nettle shoots
pulling thistles by their roots.

Father's hands
gripping like an iron vice
never numb in snow and ice
nails and screws are pulled and prised.

He once found a kestrel with a broken wing
and kept it in our garage until it was better.
He'd feed it by hand with scraps of meat or dead mice
and you could see where its beak and talons
had taken bits of skin from his finger ends.
It never seemed to hurt him at all, he just smiled
as he let it claw and peck.

Father's hands
lifting bales of hay and straw
calloused, hardened, rough and raw
building, planting, painting . . . more.

Father's hands
hard when tanning my backside
all we needed they supplied
and still my hands will fit inside

Father's hands
large like frying pans
broad as shovel blades
strong as weathered spades.

And still my hands will fit inside
my father's hands.

He Just Can't Kick It with His Foot

John Luke from our team
Is a goal-scoring machine
Phenomenally mesmerizing but . . .
The sport is called football
But his boots don't play at all
Cos he just can't kick it with his foot

He can skim it from his shin
He can spin it on his chin
He can nod it in the net with his nut
He can blow it with his lips
Or skip it off his hips
But he just can't kick it with his foot

With simplicity and ease
He can use his knobbly knees
To blast it past the keeper, both eyes shut
He can whip it up and flick it
Up with his tongue and lick it
But he just can't kick it with his foot

Overshadowing the best
With the power from his chest
Like a rocket from a socket he can put
The ball into the sack
With a scorcher from his back
But he just can't kick it with his foot

Baffling belief
With the ball between his teeth
He can dribble his way out of any rut
Hypnotize it with his eyes
Keep it up on both his thighs
But he just can't kick it with his foot

From his shoulder to his nose
He can juggle it and pose
With precision and incision he can cut
Defences straight in half
With a volley from his calf
But he just can't kick it with his foot

He can keep it off the deck
Bounce the ball upon his neck
With his ball control you should see him strut
He can flap it with both ears
To loud applause and cheers
But he just can't kick it with his foot

He can trap it with his tum
Direct it with his bum
Deflect it just by wobbling his gut
And when he's feeling silly
He can even use his . . . ankle
But he just can't kick it with his foot.

I Just Don't Trust the Furniture

I just don't trust the furniture
The desks have all got teeth
Grinning fangs inviting
Evilly delighting
At what they could be biting
And dragging down beneath . . .

Violet electric light
Bursts in violent blasts
Forked tongue lightning slithers
Like vicious neon rivers
Everybody shivers
Until the storm has passed

No one knows just how or why
But when they start to glow
When open lids are gaping
There is no escaping
The scratching and the scraping
Of the horrors down below

A corridor is opened
A gateway is unfurled
Its gravity commences
To hypnotize the senses
And drag you down defenceless
To its nightmare world

I just don't trust the furniture
The dark decaying smell
But when hungry desks are humming
Their rumbling insides drumming
Something else is coming
Beware the chairs as well . . .

I just don't trust the furniturgh . . .

Robert Burns

Robert Burns was born in Alloway, Ayshire. He was the son of a poor tenant farmer, and he later gained the nickname 'The Ploughman Poet'. He moved to Edinburgh after becoming a national celebrity, thanks to his first collection of poetry. While writing poetry and songs – over 400 songs still exist – he also earned money raising taxes. Burns is most famous for writing 'Tam O'Shanter' and 'A Red, Red Rose'. He died at the early age of thirty-seven. More than 10,000 people went to his funeral. On the anniversary of his birth – Burns Night – Scots both at home and abroad celebrate his life with a supper, where they address the haggis, the ladies, and the whisky, since all three were very close to his heart.

To a Haggis

Fair fa' your honest sonsie face,
Great chieftain o' the puddin'-race!
Aboon them a' ye tak your place,
    Painch, tripe, or thairm:
Weel are ye wordy o' a grace
    As lang's my arm.

The groaning trencher there ye fill,
Your hurdies like a distant hill;
Your pin wad help to mend a mill
    In time o' need;
While thro' your pores the dews distil
    Like amber bead.

His knife see rustic Labour dight,
An' cut you up wi' ready sleight,
Trenching your gushing entrails bright
    Like ony ditch;
And then, O what a glorious sight,
    Warm-reekin', rich!

Then, horn for horn they stretch an' strive,
Deil tak the hindmost! on they drive,
Till a' their weel-swall'd kytes belyve
    Are bent like drums;
Then auld guidman, maist like to rive,
    Bethankit hums.

Is there that o'er his French ragout,
Or olio that wad staw a sow,
Or fricassee wad mak her spew
    Wi' perfect sconner,
Looks down wi' sneering scornfu' view
    On sic a dinner?

Poor devil! See him owre his trash,
As feckless as a wither'd rash,
His spindle shank a guid whip-lash,
    His nieve a nit:
Thro' bloody flood or field to dash,
    O how unfit!

But mark the Rustic, haggis-fed –
The trembling earth resounds his tread!
Clap in his walie nieve a blade,
    He'll mak it whissle;
An' legs, an' arms, an' heads will sned,
    Like taps o' thrissle.

Ye Pow'rs, wha mak mankind your care,
And dish them out their bill o' fare,
Auld Scotland wants nae skinking ware
    That jaups in luggies;
But, if ye wish her gratefu' prayer,
    Gie her a Haggis!

To a Mouse

On turning her up in her nest with the plough, November, 1785

I

Wee, sleekit, cowrin, tim'rous beastie,
O, what a panic's in thy breastie!
Thou need na start awa sae hasty
 Wi' bickering brattle!
I wad be laith to rin an' chase thee,
 Wi' murdering pattle!

II

I'm truly sorry man's dominion
Has broken Nature's social union,
An' justifies that ill opinion
 Which makes thee startle
At me, thy poor, earth-born companion
 An' fellow mortal!

III

I doubt na, whyles, but thou may thieve;
What then? poor beastie, thou maun live.
A daimen icker in a thrave
 'S a sma' request;
I'll get a blessin wi' the lave,
 An' never miss 't!

IV

Thy wee-bit housie, too, in ruin!
Its silly wa's the win's are strewin!
An' naething, now, to big a new ane,
    O' foggage green!
An' bleak December's win's ensuin,
    Baith snell an' keen!

V

Thou saw the fields laid bare an' waste,
An' weary winter comin fast,
An' cozie here, beneath the blast,
    Thou thought to dwell,
Till crash! the cruel coulter past
    Out-thro' thy cell.

VI

That wee bit heap o' leaves an' stibble,
Hast cost thee monie a weary nibble!
Now thou's turned out, for a' thy trouble,
    But house or hald,
To thole the winter's sleety dribble,
    An' cranreuch cauld!

VII
But Mousie, thou art no thy lane,
In proving foresight may be vain:
The best-laid schemes o' mice an' men
    Gang aft agley,
An' lea'e us nought but grief an' pain,
    For promis'd joy!

VIII
Still thou art blest, compared wi' me!
The present only toucheth thee:
But och! I backward cast my e'e,
    On prospects drear!
An' forward, tho' I canna see,
    I guess an' fear!

Wednesday

Auld Lang Syne

Should auld acquaintance be forgot,
And never brought to min'?
Should auld acquaintance be forgot,
And auld lang syne?

For auld lang syne, my dear.
For auld lang syne,
We'll tak a cup o' kindness yet,
For auld lang syne.

We twa hae run about the braes,
And pu'd the gowans fine;
But we've wandered mony a weary foot
Sin' auld lang syne.

We twa hae paidled i' the burn,
From morning sun till dine;
But seas between us braid hae roared
Sin' auld lang syne.

And there's a hand, my trusty fiere,
And gie's a hand o' thine;
And we'll tak a right guid-willie waught,
For auld lang syne.

And surely ye'll be your pint-stowp,
And surely I'll be mine;
And we'll tak a cup o' kindness yet
For auld lang syne.

For auld lang syne, my dear.
For auld lang syne,
We'll take a cup o' kindness yet,
For auld lang syne.

A Red, Red Rose

O, my Luve's like a red, red rose,
  That's newly sprung in June.
Oh, my Luve's like the melodie
  That's sweetly play'd in tune.

As fair art thou, my bonnie lass,
  So deep in luve am I;
And I will love thee still, my dear,
  Till a' the seas gang dry.

Till a' the seas gang dry, my dear,
  And the rocks melt wi' the sun:
I will love thee still, my dear,
  While the sands o' life shall run:

And fare thee weel, my only luve!
  And fare thee weel, a while!
And I will come again, my luve,
  Tho' it were ten thousand mile!

My Heart's in the Highlands

My heart's in the Highlands, my heart is not here;
My heart's in the Highlands a-chasing the deer;
Chasing the wild deer, and following the roe,
My heart's in the Highlands wherever I go.
Farewell to the Highlands, farewell to the North,
The birth-place of valour, the country of worth;
Wherever I wander, wherever I rove,
The hills of the Highlands for ever I love.

Farewell to the mountains, high covered with snow;
Farewell to the straths and green valleys below;
Farewell to the forests and wild-hanging woods;
Farewell to the torrents and loud-pouring floods.
My heart's in the Highlands, my heart is not here;
My heart's in the Highlands a-chasing the deer;
Chasing the wild deer, and following the roe,
My heart's in the Highlands, wherever I go.

The Banks o' Doon

Ye flowery banks o' bonnie Doon,
  How can ye blume sae fair!
How can ye chant, ye little birds,
  And I sae fu' o' care!

Thou'll break my heart, thou bonnie bird
  That sings upon the bough;
Thou minds me o' the happy days
  When my fause Luve was true.

Thou'll break my heart, thou bonnie bird
  That sings beside thy mate;
For sae I sat, and sae I sang,
  And wist na o' my fate.

Aft hae I roved by bonnie Doon
  To see the woodbine twine,
And ilka bird sang o' its love;
  And sae did I o' mine.

Wi' lightsome heart I pu'd a rose,
  Frae aff its thorny tree;
And my fause luver staw the rose,
  But left the thorn wi' me

Bruce's Address before Bannockburn

Scots, wha hae wi' Wallace bled,
Scots, wham Bruce has aften led,
Welcome to your gory bed,
   Or to victorie.

Now's the day, and now's the hour,
See the front o' battle lour!
See approach proud Edward's power –
   Chains and slaverie!

Wha will be a traitor knave?
Wha will fill a coward's grave?
Wha sae base as be a slave?
   Let him turn and flee!

Wha for Scotland's King and law
Freedom's sword will strongly draw,
Freeman stand, or freeman fa'.
   Let him on wi' me!

By oppression's woes and pains!
By your sons in servile chains!
We will drain our dearest veins,
   But they shall be free!

Lay the proud usurpers low!
Tyrants fall in every foe!
Liberty's in every blow!
  Let us do or die!

Brian Moses

Brian Moses started writing as teenager. He tried to play the guitar and write songs, but when he realized that he wasn't going to become a rock star (which was, incidentally, some time after everyone else had come to the same conclusion) he put the guitar away and the songs turned into poems. To date, he has over 160 books published including volumes of his own poetry such as *Barking Back at Dogs* and anthologies such as *The Secret Lives of Teachers*. Brian also visits schools to run writing workshops and perform his poetry and percussion shows. He has visited well over 2,500 schools and libraries in the UK. He has made several appearances at the Edinburgh Festival, been writer in residence at Castle Cornet on Guernsey and at RAF schools in Cyprus. Recently he has visited several international schools across Europe.

Today, Brian lives in Sussex with his wife, Anne, and their two daughters, Karen and Linette. He works in a room that he had built in his garden. It is full of books, computers and percussion instruments. He has a view of lots of trees and a sheep field. At the moment the family pets are one nervous guinea pig and a hutch-wrecking bunny! They once had a lop-eared rabbit who loved to play football!

What Teachers Wear in Bed!

It's anybody's guess
what teachers wear in bed at night
so we held a competition
to see if any of us were right.

We did a spot of research,
although some of them wouldn't say,
but it's probably something funny
as they look pretty strange by day.

Our Head teacher's quite old-fashioned,
he wears a Victorian nightshirt,
our sports teacher wears her tracksuit
and sometimes her netball skirt.

That new teacher in the infants
wears bedsocks with see-through pyjamas,
our Deputy Head wears a T-shirt
he brought back from the Bahamas.

We asked our secretary what she wore
but she shooed us out of her room,
and our teacher said, her favourite nightie
and a splash of expensive perfume.

And Mademoiselle, who teaches French,
is really very rude,
she whispered, '*Alors!* Don't tell a soul,
but I sleep in the . . . back bedroom!'

Days

Days fly by on holidays,
they escape like birds
released from cages.
What a shame you can't buy
tokens of time, save them up
and lengthen the good days,
or maybe you could tear out time
from days that drag, then pay it back
on holidays, wild days,
days you wish would last forever.
You could wear these days with pride,
fasten them like poppies to your coat,
or keep them in a tin, like sweets,
a confection of days
to be held on the tongue
and tasted, now and then.

Brian Moses

Aliens Stole My Underpants

To understand the ways
of alien beings is hard,
and I've never worked it out
why they landed in my backyard.

And I've always wondered why
on their journey from the stars,
these aliens stole my underpants
and took them back to Mars.

They came on a Monday night
when the weekend wash had been done,
pegged out on the line
to be dried by the morning sun.

Mrs Driver from next door
was a witness at the scene
when aliens snatched my underpants –
I'm glad that they were clean!

It seems they were quite choosy
as nothing else was taken.
Do aliens wear underpants
or were they just mistaken?

I think I have a theory
as to what they wanted them for,
they needed to block off a draught
blowing in through the spacecraft door.

Or maybe some Mars museum
wanted items brought back from space.
Just think, my pair of Y-fronts
displayed in their own glass case.

And on the label beneath
would be written where they got 'em
and how such funny underwear
once covered an Earthling's bottom!

Make Friends with a Tree

Give a tree a squeeze,
give a tree a hug,
join in celebration
with every bird and bug,

with every bat and badger,
with beetles and with bees,
a new year's resolution,
show kindness to the trees.

Make friends with a tree,
make friends with a tree,
hug a tree, go on show it
you really care, let a tree know it.
Make friends with a tree,
make friends with a tree.

Trees are always homes
to every sort of creature.
In a flat and empty landscape
a tree is a special feature.

Trees can be deciduous,
pine trees are coniferous,
but trees will never hurt you
no tree is carnivorous!

So treat a tree politely,
show it you're sincere.
Long after we have disappeared
trees will still be here.

Make friends with a tree,
make friends with a tree,
hug a tree, go on show it
you really care, let a tree know it.
Make friends with a tree,
make friends with a tree.

Snuggle up to a sycamore,
cuddle up to a pine,
wrap your arms around an oak,
enjoy a joke with a lime.

A tree will always listen,
tell your troubles to a tree.
To the mystery of life
an ash may hold the key.

So don't be abrupt with a birch,
don't try to needle a pine.
Don't interrupt a horse chestnut,
don't give a tree a hard time.

Make friends with a tree,
make friends with a tree,
hug a tree, go on show it
you really care, let a tree know it.
Make friends with a tree,
make friends with a tree.

A tree is a living thing,
it's not just a lump of wood.
Trees in Sherwood Forest
know all about Robin Hood.

A tree can tell us stories,
a tree knows history,
so in this world of fake and sham
let's celebrate truth in a tree.

Make friends with a tree,
make friends with a tree,
hug a tree, go on show it
you really care, let a tree know it.
Make friends with a tree,
make friends with a tree.

All the Things You Can Say to Places in the UK

Always say 'Ta' to Leamington Spa,
say 'Have a nice day' to Whitley Bay.
You can shout 'What's new' or even 'Howdoo'
to inhabitants of Looe or Crewe.
You can tell the whole story in Tobermory,
say 'Hi' to Rye and 'Right on' to Brighton,
or call out 'Let's go' to Plymouth Ho.
Talk through your dreams in Milton Keynes,
say 'It's all for the best' in Haverfordwest.
Always say 'Yes' when you visit Skegness
but only say 'No' in Llandudno.
Don't tell a lie to the Island of Skye
or say 'It smells' in Tunbridge Wells.
Don't talk rude if you're down in Bude
or start to get gabby in Waltham Abbey.
Don't ever plead in Berwick on Tweed
or say 'You look ill' to Burgess Hill.
You could lose your voice and talk with your hands
when you take a trip to Camber Sands,
but whatever you say just won't impress
the residents of Shoeburyness.

Lost Magic

Today I found some lost magic –
a twisty-twirly horn
of a unicorn lying at my feet.
And when I stopped
to pick it up, to hold it
in my fist, I remembered
how once upon a time
you could always find unicorns,
but there are no unicorns now.

You would find them on the shoreline,
flitting in and out of caves in cliffs,
or climbing hills at twilight.
They would lead you through forests,
sometimes hiding behind trees,
and if you lost them or they lost you,
you could always find them again,
but there are no unicorns now.

And it didn't matter
if you followed them all day,
the edge of the world was miles away,
there was nothing to fear.
And none of the unicorns we knew ever
changed into dangerous strangers.

Once upon a time there *were* unicorns
but there are no unicorns now.

A Feather from an Angel

Anton's box of treasures held
a silver key and a glassy stone,
a figurine made of polished bone
and a feather from an angel.

The figurine was from Borneo,
the stone from France or Italy,
the silver key was a mystery
but the feather came from an angel.

We might have believed him if he'd said
the feather fell from a bleached white crow
but he always replied, 'It's an angel's, I know,
a feather from an angel.'

We might have believed him if he'd said,
'An albatross let the feather fall.'
But he had no doubt, no doubt at all,
his feather came from an angel.

'I thought I'd dreamt him one night,' he'd say,
'but in the morning I knew he'd been there;
he left a feather on my bedside chair,
a feather from an angel.'

And it seems that all my life I've looked
for the sort of belief that nothing could shift,
something simple and precious as Anton's gift,
a feather from an angel.

Jenny Joseph

Jenny Joseph was born in Birmingham in 1932, but her first remembered home was in leafy Buckinghamshire on the edge of the Chilterns not far from the Thames. Other important childhood places were Dorset (she learned to ride a bicycle the winter Poole Harbour froze over), and later, the North Devon coast. Books have always been important to her. She left school when she was fifteen and went abroad to learn languages. Later she got a scholarship to Oxford. Jenny has done a variety of jobs from cleaning to teaching to being the landlady of a public house. She has written books for children and adults in prose and verse, and has collaborated with musicians and painters. Among the many things she would have liked to learn to do, but can't, are science, film-making and building.

Jenny Joseph

The magic of the brain

Such a sight I saw:
An eight-sided kite surging up into a cloud
Its eight tails streaming out as if they were one.
It lifted my heart as starlight lifts the head
Such a sight I saw.

And such a sound I heard:
One bird through dim winter light as the day was closing
Poured out a song suddenly from an empty tree.
It cleared my head as water refreshes the skin
Such a sound I heard.

Such a smell I smelled:
A mixture of roses and coffee, of green leaf and warmth.
It took me to gardens and summer and cities abroad,
Memories of meetings as if my past friends were here
Such a smell I smelled.

Such soft fur I felt:
It wrapped me around, soothing my winter-cracked skin,
Not gritty or stringy or sweaty but silkily warm
As my animal slept on my lap, and we both breathed
    content
Such soft fur I felt.

Such food I tasted:
Smooth-on-tongue soup, and juicy crackling of meat,
Greens like fresh fields, sweet-on-your-palate peas,
Jellies and puddings and fragrance of fruit they are
   made from
Such good food I tasted.

Such a world comes in:
Far world of the sky to breathe in through your nose
Near world you feel underfoot as you walk on the land.
Through your eyes and your ears and your mouth
   and your brilliant brain
Such a world comes in.

Jenny Joseph

Having visitors

I heard you were coming and
Thrum thrum thrum
Went something in my heart like a
Drum drum drum.

I briskly walked down the
Street street street
To buy lovely food for us to
Eat eat eat.

I cleaned the house and filled it with
Flowers flowers flowers
And asked the sun to drink up the
Showers showers showers.

Steadily purring
Thrum, thrum, thrum
Went the drum in my heart because
You'd come, come, come.

Ugh!

Grubby little feet
Where have you been?
Don't you bring all that dirt in
My carpet's clean.

Sticky little hands
What's squashed up in them?
Have you taken fistfuls oozing
With butter and jam?

Dribbly chocolate mouth
(Cat that's lapped the cream)
Don't you rub your itchy face
On my arm.

Into the bath with you!
Now I can see your face.
Itch and dirt away it goes
Sand from in between your toes
Down the plughole with the water
Now there's splashing and there's laughter

And warm clean healthy feet.

Jenny Joseph

The things I see

Hurry hurry hurry
It won't do you no good though.
The lights ahead are red
You go up to them slap bang
Rocking on your chassis.
Meanwhile you have missed
What I have seen –
A small boy hiding behind a tree
And the buds breaking out all around him, kissed
With little tongues of green.

Angry angry angry.
It won't do you no good though
For the catch on the door will slide
When you push your boxes through at that hasty angle.
The red fuming skin of your face
Must be all your eyes can see.
Meanwhile you have missed
What I have seen –
A woman with a strange patched face
Looking up into the spring sky through the mist
In her light eyes for Heaven's Queen.

Furry furry furry
It won't do you much good though
To be wrapped so warm to the eyes
That you cannot turn your head
That you miss what I have seen –
All the things I see:
A tall man like a pole
And at the bottom of his long arms, down at his feet
A tiny little pushchair and a tiny baby
Sunk in its hammocky seat between the wheels;
A little girl sitting high up on her father's arm
With a long furry tail laid heavy among her ringlets
Swinging from her Davy Crockett hat;
And two extraordinary pigeons
Of quite different and glistening colours.
And a cloak of St Francis brown and a Mary's blue
Walking together, collecting the dust of the street
All the things that I see
As I hurry hurry hurry
To work, but slowly, slowly.

Jenny Joseph

The life of feet

Walking, walking down by the sea
Walking, walking up on the hill
Strong feet, long feet
Squat feet, young feet
     Making tracks on paths
     Shuffling through the leaves
     Going with a purpose

     Feeling the sand and the waves
     Knowing the grass and the land.

     Running, running in through the gate
     Clattering, jumping, up to the steps
Shapely feet, firm feet
Straight feet, tired feet
     Coming home after play
     Up the steps to the door
     Glad to have a rest

     Warmed by the sand, soothed by the waves
     Cooled by the grass, firmed by the land

Good strong walking feet.

Getting back home

Hang your hat on the peg
Rest up, rest up
Fling your coat on the bed
For you have travelled many miles to see me.

Put your feet on the bench
Rest up, rest up
Heave off your heavy boots
For you have come through winter days to see me.

Settle down by the fire
Rest up, rest up
Lean back and smile at me
For after all this time and travelling
Oh traveller, I'm glad to see you.

Another story of Red Riding Hood

I know a girl who's fit to eat
I know a girl with good strong feet
For walking;
I know a girl with sparkly eyes
I know a girl who doesn't tell lies,
My darling.

I know a wolf in a forest lair
Plotting and planning with great care
For dinner
To trick a girl who's thoughtful and kind.
It's always in her Grandma's mind
To win her

Away from the dangers of the wood
And keep her safe if only she could
Protect her.
The wolf is slinking through the trees
And he must hurry if he's
To collect her.

The girl, too sensible to stay
And dilly-dally on the way,
Was singing.
Her bag held her and Granny's luncheon
From it her father's hawthorn truncheon
Was swinging.

This was the song that she sang to the wolf
To the hungry wolf who grumbled and snarled:

You are bad and I am good
You stay in your part of the wood,
I'll keep my way.
You can have my sandwiches for lunch
(They're juicier than Gran's bones to munch).
Then go away.

She shouted and waved her stick and danced
And the wolf saw a pigeon, as it chanced,
Deep in the wood.
Thinking as always about her Gran
Like a mile-a-minute sprinter ran
Red Riding Hood.

Grace Nichols

Grace Nichols was born in Guyana, West Indies, in 1950. She came to Britain in 1977. Her books include novels for children and adults, and collections of poetry. Her cycle of poems *I Is a Long Memoried Woman* was published in 1983 and won the Commonwealth Poetry Prize. Her children's books include *Come On In To My Tropical Garden*, *Give Yourself a Hug* and *The Poet's Cat*. She was Poet in Residence at the Tate Gallery from 1999–2000. This provided the inspiration for her most recent book, *Paint Me a Poem*. With her partner, John Agard, she co-edited the anthology *Under the Moon and Over the Sea*, which received the first CLPE Children's Poetry Award.

Morning

Morning comes
  with a milk-float jiggling

Morning comes
  with a milkman whistling

Morning comes
  with empties clinking

Morning comes
  with alarm-clock ringing

Morning comes
  with toaster popping

Morning comes
  with letters dropping

Morning comes
  with kettle singing

Morning comes
  with me just listening

Morning comes to drag me out of bed
  – Boss-Woman Morning.

Grace Nichols

For Forest

Forest could keep secrets
Forest could keep secrets

Forest tune in every day
to watersound and birdsound
Forest letting her hair down
to the teeming creeping of her forest-ground

But Forest don't broadcast her business
no Forest cover her business down
from sky and fast-eye sun
and when night come
and darkness wrap her like a gown
Forest is a bad dream woman

Forest dreaming about mountain
and when earth was young
Forest dreaming of the caress of gold
Forest rootsing with mysterious Eldorado

and when howler monkey
wake her up with howl
Forest just stretch and stir
to a new day of sound

but coming back to secrets
Forest could keep secrets
Forest could keep secrets

And we must keep Forest

Mama-Wata

Down by the seaside
when the moon is in bloom
sits Mama-Wata
gazing up at the moon

She sits as she combs
her hair like a loom
she sits as she croons
a sweet kind of tune

But don't go near Mama-Wata
when the moon is in bloom
for sure she will take you
down to your doom.

Grace Nichols

Give Yourself a Hug

Give yourself a hug
when you feel unloved

Give yourself a hug
when people put on airs
to make you feel a bug

Give yourself a hug
when everyone seems to give you
a cold-shoulder shrug

Give yourself a hug –
a big big hug

And keep on singing,
'Only one in a million like me
Only one in a million-billion-thrillion-zillion
like me.'

Granny Granny
Please Comb My Hair

Granny Granny please comb my hair
you always take your time
you always take such care

You put me on a cushion between your knees
you rub a little coconut oil
parting gentle as a breeze

Mummy Mummy
she's always in a hurry-hurry
rush
she pulls my hair
sometimes she tugs

But Granny
you have all the time
in the world
and when you're finished
you always turn my head and say
'Now who's a nice girl?'

Tabby

My cat is all concentrated tiger.
I can only imagine the thousands
of millions of years
it must have taken to perfect her.
Growing smaller and smaller
with each evolution.
Growing more and more refined
and even-tempered under her fur.

See how she constantly licks
and grooms herself all over?

A small Queen of Sheba
stamping everywhere her padded
signature – a royal reminder
of the days she was a full-blown tiger.
Older O much older than Egypt.

Now, just look at her –
my grey and black tabby, stepping lightly,
emerging head first from between
the green garden stalks –

Ancient and new as the birth of a star.

Teenage Earthbirds

Flying by
on the winged-wheels
of their heels

Two teenage earthbirds
skate-boarding
down the street

Rising
unfeathered –
in sudden air-leap

Defying law
death and gravity
as they do a wheelie

Landing back
in the smooth swoop
of youth

And faces gaping
gawking, impressed
and unimpressed

Only mother watches – heartbeat in her mouth.

Carol Ann Duffy

Carol Ann Duffy was born in Glasgow in 1955. She grew up in Stafford. During the 1970s she studied philosophy at the University of Liverpool. During the 1980s she lived in London, working as a writer-in-residence in East End schools before becoming a full-time writer and dramatist in 1985.

She has received many awards for her collections, including both the Forward and the Whitbread for *Mean Time* in 1993. Her last collection, *The World's Wife*, was in the top five best-selling poetry titles in 1999. The book was shortlisted in the collections' category for the Forward Poetry Prize.

Her books for children include *Meeting Midnight*, which was shortlisted for the Whitbread Prize and *Oldest Girl in the World*, which won the Signal Award for Poetry, and, most recently, *The Good Child's Guide to Rock 'n' Roll*.

She lives in Manchester with her daughter, Ella, where she lectures on poetry for the Writing School at Manchester Metropolitan University.

Teacher

When you teach me,
your hands bless the air
where chalk dust sparkles.

And when you talk,
the six wives of Henry VIII
stand in the room like bridesmaids,

or the Nile drifts past the classroom window,
the Pyramids baking like giant cakes
on the playing fields.

You teach with your voice,
so a tiger prowls from a poem
and pads between desks, black and gold

in the shadow and sunlight,
or the golden apples of the sun drop
from a branch in my mind's eye.

I bow my head again
to this tattered, doodled book
and learn what love is.

Carol Ann Duffy

Sharp Freckles

(for Ben Simmons)

He picks me up, his big thumbs under my armpits tickle,
then puts me down. On his belt there is a shining silver
   buckle.
I hold his hand and see, close up, the dark hairs on his
   knuckles.

He sings to me. His voice is loud and funny and I giggle.
Now we will eat. I listen to my breakfast as it crackles.
He nods and smiles. His eyes are birds in little nests of
   wrinkles.

We kick a ball, red and white, between us. When he tackles
I'm on the ground, breathing a world of grass. It prickles.
He bends. He lifts me high above his head. Frightened, I
   wriggle.

Face to face, I watch the sweat above each caterpillar-
   eyebrow trickle.
He rubs his nose on mine, once, twice, three times, and we
   both chuckle.
He hasn't shaved today. He kisses me. He has sharp
   freckles.

Dimples

When I'm scared the Monsters are thrilling me.
When I'm cold the North Wind is chilling me.
When I'm pretty some ribbons are frilling me.
When I'm fibbing my teacher is grilling me.
When I'm sad my salt tears are spilling free.
When I'm brave my courage is willing me.
When I fidget my Grandma is stilling me.
When I'm hungry my Mother is filling me.
When I'm spending the toy shop is billing me.
When I score the referee's nilling me.
When I'm ill the doctor is pilling me.
When it's dawn the sparrows are trilling me.
But when I laugh and laugh and laugh and laugh
and laugh MY DIMPLES ARE KILLING ME!

Carol Ann Duffy

The Oldest Girl in the World

Children, I remember how I could hear
with my soft young ears
the tiny sounds of the air –
tinkles and chimes
like minuscule bells
ringing continually there;
clinks and chinks
like glasses of sparky gooseberry wine,
jolly and glinting and raised in the air.
Yes, I could hear like a bat. And how!
Can't hear a sniff of it now.

Truly, believe me, I could all the time see
every insect that crawled in a bush,
every bird that hid in a tree,
individually.
If I wanted to catch a caterpillar
to keep as a pet in a box
I had only to watch a cabbage
and there it would be,
crawling bendy and green towards me.
Yes, I could see with the eyes of a cat. Miaow!
Can't see a sniff of it now.

And my sense of taste was second to none.
By God, the amount I knew with my tongue!
The shrewd taste of a walnut's brain.
The taste of a train from a bridge.
Of a kiss. Of air chewy with midge.
Of fudge from a factory two miles away
from the house where I lived.
I'd stick out my tongue
to savour the sky in a droplet of rain.
Yes, I could taste like the fang of a snake! Wow!
Can't taste a sniff of it now.

On the scent, what couldn't I smell
with my delicate nose, my nostrils of pearl?
I could smell the world!
Snow. Soot. Soil.
Satsumas in their Christmas sock.
The ink of a pen.
The stink of an elephant's skin.
The blue broth of a swimming pool. Dive in!
The showbizzy gasp of the wind.
Yes, I could smell like a copper's dog. Bow-wow!
Can't smell a sniff of it now.

As for my sense of touch
it was too much!
The cold of a snowball
felt through the vanishing heat of a mitt.
A peach like an apple wearing a vest.
The raffia dish of a bird's nest
A hot chestnut
branding the palm at the heart of the fist.
The stab of the thorn on the rose. Long grass, its itch.
Yes, I could feel with the sensitive hand of a ghost.
    Whooo!
Can't feel a sniff of it now.

Can't see a
Can't hear a
Can't taste a
Can't smell a
Can't feel a bit of it whiff of it niff of it.
Can't get a sniff of it now.

A Week as My Home Town

Monday:
Rain. I'm the Library, round-shouldered, my stone brow
frowning at pigeons, my windows steamed up
like spectacles, my swing doors tut-tutting, my bricks
beginning to feel the damp.
                                   Readers come,
whispering and coughing, shaking umbrellas
at the back of my yawning marble throat. My old lifts sigh
up and down, up and down, up and down. *Sssssshhh.*

Books flap in my head like birds.

Tuesday:
Weak sun. I'm the Park. My trees
wear last night's rain like jewels.
I shake birds from my hair as I wake, gargle
with a water-fountain, admire my green face
in the mirror of a small lake.
                                   My thoughts
are a game of bowls, slow and calm.
I hum to myself in a lawnmower bass
among my bright municipal flowers,
my namesake benches.

Wednesday:
Fog. Museum, me. I hark back
to the past for endless hours, hoard
bronze coins in glass wallets, keep
long-gone summer butterflies on pins.

I remember things, pick
over old bones, look under cold stones,
check the names of the Kings and Queens
who sat on the gold thrones.

My stained-glass eyes stare inwards.

Thursday:
Sunshine. I'm the Main Road.
I lie on my back, stretch out
my side-street arms, wriggle
my alley toes, my mews fingers.

My throat is a tunnel
under a river. I burp cars
into the sparkling daylight,
belch lorries and juggernauts.

My heart's a roundabout,
in love with the next town.

Friday:
Grey cloud. I'm the Cinema, daydream
all day, can't sleep at night, hear

voices . . . *to infinity and beyond* . . . see
faces . . . *I'm all aloooone* . . . smell

popcorn . . . *please sir, can I have
some more* . . . They shine a light

in my eyes, prod at my plush red teeth.
I want to phone home. I'll be right here.

Saturday:
Frost. I'm the Disco. My neon lips
pout at the shivery night. My heart thumps
so loud the queue outside can hear it.

I wear light, glitterballs, lasers, strobe,
too much perfume. One day I'll give up smoking.
If anyone asks if I'm dancing, I'm dancing.

Sunday:
Snow. I'm the Church,
stone-flags for my shoes,
for my hat a steeple.

I kneel by the side of the graves
and sob with my bells.
Where are the people?

Carol Ann Duffy

Meeting Midnight

I met Midnight.
Her eyes were sparkling pavements after frost.
She wore a full-length, dark blue raincoat with a hood.
She winked. She smoked a small cheroot.

I followed her.
Her walk was more a shuffle, more a dance.
She took the path to the river, down she went.
On Midnight's scent,
I heard the twelve cool syllables, her name,
chime from the town.
When those bells stopped,

Midnight paused by the water's edge.
She waited there.
I saw a girl in purple on the bridge.
It was One O'Clock.
Hurry, Midnight said, *it's late, it's late*.
I saw them run together.
Midnight wept.
They kissed full on the lips
and then I slept.

The next day I bumped into Half-Past Four.
He was a bore.

The Giantess

Where can I find seven small girls to be pets,
where can I find them?
One to comb the long grass of my hair
with this golden rake,
one to dig with this copper spade
the dirt from under my nails.
I will pay them in crab-apples.

Where can I find seven small girls to help me,
where can I find them?
A third to scrub at my tombstone teeth
with this mop in its bronze bucket,
a fourth to scoop out the wax from my ears
with this platinum trowel.
I will pay them in yellow pears.

Where can I find seven small girls to be good dears,
where can I find them?
A fifth one to clip the nails of my toes
with these sharp silver shears,
a sixth to blow my enormous nose
with this satin sheet.
I will pay them in plums.

But the seventh girl will stand on the palm of my hand,
singing and dancing,
and I will love the tiny music of her voice,
her sweet little jigs.
I will pay her in grapes and kumquats and figs.
Where can I find her?
Where can I find seven small girls to be pets?

Peter Dixon

When Peter Dixon was at school he wasn't much good at reading and writing and all that stuff. In fact, he was pretty awful. He was miles better at wall climbing and mucking around with his pals. He also liked boxing. When he was eleven years old he fought a champion called Bobbie Dunn. Peter only weighed seventy-four pounds, so he's grown a bit since then, and he's got a beard. Quite a few poets were boxers – Vernon Scannell, Lord Byron, Robert Graves, and of course Muhammad Ali!

Peter hates homework, SATs tests, emptying Hoovers, getting up in the morning, and next door's cat (because it catches birds). He earns his living running courses for teachers, visiting schools and, of course, writing stories and poems. He also paints, and exhibits his work mostly in Cornwall.

As he was so bad at spelling, adverbs, clauses and comprehension exercises, you might be surprised to hear that Peter became a writer, a teacher and a senior lecturer in education. Phew! He doesn't quite know how all that happened. It just did . . . he thinks it was something to do with playing a lot (he still plays!) – and thinking up good ideas that no one else has thought of. Instead of copying things out, or copying Mr Monet's water gardens, he goes and discovers his own things to write about and paint – odd things sometimes; strange or sad, happy or silly. Anyway, he'll tell you all about it and help you all to write even better poems and stories if and when he ever visits your schools, libraries, conferences, festivals – whenever and wherever.

Peter Dixon

Chair Boy

Mavis Thompson's Mary,
    Julian's a king,
Geoffrey Jones is Joseph
    but I'm not anything.

Last year I was a palm tree,
    the year before a goat
and when I was in playgroup
    I wore a shepherd's coat.

But now I am a junior
    and cannot learn by heart,
I'll always be a chair boy
    and I'll never get a part.

I'll never be a wise man
an inn man
or a sage . . .
But I'll always be important
    in a place that's called
        backstage.

Lone Mission

On evenings, after cocoa
(blackout down and sealed)
I would build plasticine Hamburgs
on green lino
and bomb them with encyclopaedias
(dropped at ceiling level)
from my Lancaster Bomber
built
(usually)
from table, box and curtains
turret made of chairs
radio and gas masks
tray and kitchen ware.
But:
     Aircrew were my problem
     gunners mid and rear
     radio and bomber
     nav. and engineer.

Each night I flew lone missions
through flak both hot and wild
and learnt it wasn't easy
to be an only child.

Peter Dixon

My Daddy Dances Tapstep

Roger's Daddy's clever
Daisy's flies a plane
Michael's does computers
And has a house in Spain.
Lucy's goes to London
He stays there every week . . .
  But my Daddy has an earring
    and lovely dancing feet.

He hasn't got a briefcase
He hasn't got a phone
He hasn't got a mortgage
And we haven't got a home.
He hasn't got a fax machine
We haven't got a car
  But he can dance and fiddle
    And my Daddy is
      A Star.

Tick

Mum says
    Mick
        has a tick

But I can't
    hear
        anything

Peter Dixon

Poem (after PE lesson)

And now it's time for sensible time,
Everyone on the sensible mat . . .
that's better,
that's much better.
Wayne! We are all having sensible time.
That means you too.
We are not having pushing and tugging of people time . . .
Now we all know why we are sitting here, don't we?
No, Jamie, it's nothing to do with football
– or your uncle, Hannah.
We are all sitting here because
we have a very important visitor.
We are also sitting here because Paul has lost his trousers . . .
and now the poetry man has got to wait
until the person who is wearing Paul's trousers
owns up.
Now let's all look carefully.
Someone is wearing Paul's trousers.
The poetry man must think we are all very silly children.
No, Liza, of course the poetry man hasn't taken Paul's
trousers.
If we go on being silly
and if we continue wasting the poetry man's time,
he will never read to us
and he will never explain
where he gets all his clever ideas from.

Wildlife

Why do we say wildlife
when wildlife isn't wild?
    It's mostly soft and gentle,
    it's mostly meek and mild.
We don't see lions bombing
and tigers driving tanks,
platoons of pink flamingos
or regiments of yaks.
We don't see wars of blue whales
or rabbits flying jets,
walruses with shotguns
or parachuting pets.
To me wildlife is gentle
it loves to hide away,
it's mostly shy and silent
it likes to run and play.
    It's really us that's wildlife
    our lifestyle's really wild
    bombs
    and bangs
    and burnings
    father, mother, child.

Peter Dixon

Grown-Ups

Where are your trainers and where is your coat
Where is your pen and where are your books
Where is the paper and where is the key
Where is the sugar and where is the tea
Where are your socks
Your bag and your hat?
Tidy your room!
Look after the cat!

You're hopeless
Untidy
You lose everything.

Where is your bracelet and where is your ring
Where is your ruler
Hymn book and shoes
Where is your scarf?
You lose and you lose.

You're hopeless
Untidy
You lose everything.

You're careless and casual
You drop and you fling
You're destructive and thoughtless
You don't seem to care
Your coat's on the floor
Your boots on the chair
Why don't you think
Why don't you try
Learn to be helpful; like your father and I.

Mum . . . Dad . . .

Where are the woodlands, the corncrake and the whales
Where are all the dolphins, the tigers and dales
Where are the Indians, the buffalo herds
Fishes and forests and great flying birds

Where are the rivers
Where are the seas
Where are the marshes
And where are the trees

Where is the pure air
Acid-free showers
Where are the moorlands
The meadows and flowers?

These were your treasures
Your keepsakes of time
You've lost them
You've sold them
And they could have been mine.

Lewis Carroll

Charles Lutwidge Dodgson, otherwise known as Lewis Carroll, was the son of a vicar and spent his childhood in Cheshire and Yorkshire. It was at Oxford University that he wrote his famous books about Alice, and it is the poems that can be found in the Alice books that are his most humorous and popular.

Jabberwocky

'Twas brillig, and the slithy toves
    Did gyre and gimble in the wabe;
All mimsy were the borogoves,
    And the mome raths outgrabe.

'Beware the Jabberwock, my son!
    The jaws that bite, the claws that catch!
Beware the Jubjub bird, and shun
    The frumious Bandersnatch!'

He took his vorpal sword in hand:
    Long time the manxome foe he sought –
So rested he by the Tumtum tree,
    And stood awhile in thought.

And as in uffish thought he stood,
    The Jabberwock, with eyes of flame,
Came whiffling through the tulgey wood,
    And burbled as it came!

One, two! One, two! And through and through
    The vorpal blade went snicker-snack!
He left it dead, and with its head
    He went galumphing back.

'And hast thou slain the Jabberwock?
  Come to my arms, my beamish boy!
O frabjous day! Callooh! Callay!'
  He chortled in his joy.

'Twas brillig, and the slithy toves
  Did gyre and gimble in the wabe;
All mimsy were the borogoves,
  And the mome raths outgrabe.

Tuesday

Twinkle Twinkle, Little Bat

Twinkle, twinkle, little bat!
How I wonder what you're at!
Up above the world you fly,
Like a tea-tray in the sky.
  Twinkle, twinkle –
Twinkle, twinkle, twinkle, twinkle.

You Are Old, Father William

'You are old, Father William,' the young man said,
'And your hair has become very white;
And yet you incessantly stand on your head –
Do you think, at your age, it is right?'

'In my youth,' Father William replied to his son,
'I feared it might injure the brain;
But, now that I'm perfectly sure I have none,
Why, I do it again and again.'

'You are old,' said the youth, 'as I mentioned before,
And have grown most uncommonly fat;
Yet you turned a back-somersault in at the door –
Pray, what is the reason of that?'

'In my youth,' said the sage, as he shook his grey locks,
'I kept all my limbs very supple
By the use of this ointment – one shilling the box –
Allow me to sell you a couple?'

'You are old,' said the youth, 'and your jaws are too weak
For anything tougher than suet;
Yet you finished the goose, with the bones and the beak –
Pray, how did you manage to do it?'

'In my youth,' said his father, 'I took to the law,
And argued each case with my wife;
And the muscular strength, which it gave to my jaw,
Has lasted the rest of my life.'

'You are old,' said the youth, 'one would hardly suppose
That your eye was as steady as ever;
Yet you balanced an eel on the end of your nose –
What made you so awfully clever?'

'I have answered three questions, and that is enough,'
Said his father. 'Don't give yourself airs!
Do you think I can listen all day to such stuff?
Be off, or I'll kick you downstairs!'

The Lobster-Quadrille

'Will you walk a little faster?' said a whiting to a snail,
'There's a porpoise close behind us, and he's treading on my
  tail.
See how eagerly the lobsters and the turtles all advance!
They are waiting on the shingle – will you come and join the
  dance?
  Will you, won't you, will you, won't you, will you join
    the dance?
  Will you, won't you, will you, won't you, won't you join
    the dance?

'You can really have no notion how delightful it will be
When they take us up and throw us, with the lobsters, out
  to sea!'
But the snail replied 'Too far, too far!' and gave a look
  askance –
Said he thanked the whiting kindly; but he would not join
  the dance.
  Would not, could not, would not, could not, would not
    join the dance.
  Would not, could not, would not, could not, could not
    join the dance.

'What matters it how far we go?' his scaly friend replied.
'There is another shore, you know, upon the other side.
The further off from England the nearer is to France –
Then turn not pale, beloved snail, but come and join the
    dance.
    Will you, won't you, will you, won't you, will you join
      the dance?
    Will you, won't you, will you, won't you, won't you join
      the dance?'

Lewis Carroll

The Walrus and the Carpenter

The sun was shining on the sea,
Shining with all his might:
He did his very best to make
The billows smooth and bright –
And this was odd, because it was
The middle of the night.

The moon was shining sulkily,
Because she thought the sun
Had got no business to be there
After the day was done –
'It's very rude of him,' she said,
'To come and spoil the fun!'

The sea was wet as wet could be,
The sands were dry as dry.
You could not see a cloud, because
No cloud was in the sky:
No birds were flying overhead –
There were no birds to fly.

The Walrus and the Carpenter
Were walking close at hand;
They wept like anything to see
Such quantities of sand;
'If this were only cleared away,'
They said, 'it *would* be grand!'

'If seven maids with seven mops
Swept it for half a year,
Do you suppose,' the Walrus said,
'That they could get it clear?'
'I doubt it,' said the Carpenter,
And shed a bitter tear.

'O Oysters, come and walk with us!'
The Walrus did beseech.
'A pleasant walk, a pleasant talk,
Along the briny beach:
We cannot do with more than four,
To give a hand to each.'

The eldest Oyster looked at him,
But never a word he said:
The eldest Oyster winked his eye,
And shook his heavy head –
Meaning to say he did not choose
To leave the oyster-bed.

But four young Oysters hurried up,
All eager for the treat:
Their coats were brushed, their faces washed,
Their shoes were clean and neat –
And this was odd, because, you know,
They hadn't any feet.

Four other Oysters followed them,
And yet another four;
And thick and fast they came at last,
And more, and more, and more –
All hopping through the frothy waves,
And scrambling to the shore.

The Walrus and the Carpenter
Walked on a mile or so,
And then they rested on a rock
Conveniently low:
And all the little Oysters stood
And waited in a row.

'The time has come,' the Walrus said,
'To talk of many things:
Of shoes – and ships – and sealing wax –
Of cabbages – and kings –
And why the sea is boiling hot –
And whether pigs have wings.'

'But wait a bit,' the Oysters cried,
'Before we have our chat;
For some of us are out of breath,
And all of us are fat!'
'No hurry!' said the Carpenter.
They thanked him much for that.

'A loaf of bread,' the Walrus said,
'Is what we chiefly need;
Pepper and vinegar besides
Are very good indeed –
Now, if you're ready, Oysters dear,
We can begin to feed.'

'But not on us,' the Oysters cried,
Turning a little blue.
'After such kindness that would be
A dismal thing to do!'
'The night is fine,' the Walrus said,
'Do you admire the view?'

'It was so kind of you to come,
And you are very nice!'
The Carpenter said nothing but,
'Cut us another slice.
I wish you were not quite so deaf –
I've had to ask you twice!'

'It seems a shame,' the Walrus said,
'To play them such a trick.
After we've brought them out so far
And made them trot so quick!'
The Carpenter said nothing but,
'The butter's spread too thick!'

'I weep for you,' the Walrus said,
'I deeply sympathize.'
With sobs and tears he sorted out
Those of the largest size,
Holding his pocket-handkerchief
Before his streaming eyes.

'O Oysters,' said the Carpenter,
'You've had a pleasant run!
Shall we be trotting home again?'
But answer came there none –
And this was scarcely odd, because
They'd eaten every one.

How doth the little crocodile

How doth the little crocodile
   Improve his shining tail,
And pour the waters of the Nile
   On every golden scale!

How cheerfully he seems to grin,
   How neatly spreads his claws,
And welcomes little fishes in
   With gently smiling jaws!

Lewis Carroll

Beautiful Soup

Beautiful Soup, so rich and green,
　Waiting in a hot tureen!
Who for such dainties would not stoop?
Soup of the evening, beautiful Soup!
Soup of the evening, beautiful Soup!
　Beau-ootiful Soo-oop!
　Beau-ootiful Soo-oop!
Soo-oop of the e-e-evening,
　Beautiful, beautiful Soup!

Beautiful Soup! Who cares for fish,
　Game, or any other dish?
Who would not give all else for two p
ennyworth only of beautiful Soup?
Pennyworth only of beautiful Soup?
　Beau-ootiful Soo-oop!
　Beau-ootiful Soo-oop!
Soo-oop of the e-e-evening,
　Beautiful, beauti-FUL SOUP!

James Berry

James was born in a north-east coastal village in Portland, Jamaica, West Indies. He went to work on farms in the USA in the 1940s and then came to live in England in 1948.

He started developing his writing while he worked as an international telegraphist for British Telecom. He is the author of a number of poetry collections for children and adults and he won the Signal Poetry Award for his collection *When I Dance* in 1989. His selected poems for children *Only One of Me* has recently been published.

James Berry

When I Dance

When I dance it isn't merely
That music absorbs my shyness,
My laughter settles in my eyes,
My swings of arms convert my frills
As timing tunes my feet with floor
As if I never just looked on.

It is that when I dance
O music expands my hearing
And it wants no mathematics,
It wants no thinking, no speaking,
It only wants all my feeling
In with animation of place.

When I dance it isn't merely
That surprises dictate movements,
Other rhythms move my rhythms,
I uncradle rocking-memory
And skipping, hopping and running
All mix movements I balance in.

It is that when I dance
I'm costumed in a rainbow mood,
I'm okay at any angle,
Outfit of drums crowds madness round,
Talking winds and plucked strings conspire,
Beat after beat warms me like sun.

When I dance it isn't merely
I shift bodyweight balances
As movement amasses my show,
I celebrate each dancer here,
No sleep invades me now at all
And I see how I am tireless.

It is that when I dance
I gather up all my senses
Well into hearing and feeling,
With body's flexible postures
Telling their poetry in movement
And I celebrate all rhythms.

James Berry

One

Only one of me
and nobody can get a second one
from a photocopy machine.

Nobody has the fingerprints I have.
Nobody can cry my tears, or laugh my laugh
or have my expectancy when I wait.

But anybody can mimic my dance with my dog.
Anybody can howl how I sing out of tune.
And mirrors can show me multiplied
many times, say, dressed up in red
or dressed up in grey.

Nobody can get into my clothes for me
or feel my fall for me, or do my running.
Nobody hears my music for me, either.

I am just this one.
Nobody else makes the words
I shape with sound, when I talk.

But anybody can act how I stutter in a rage.
Anybody can copy echoes I make.
And mirrors can show me multiplied
many times, say, dressed up in green
or dressed up in blue.

Playing a Dazzler

You bash drums playing a dazzler;
I worry a trumpet swaying with it.

You dance, you make a girl's skirt swirl;
I dance, I dance by myself.

You bowl, I lash air and my wicket;
I bowl, you wallop boundary balls.

Your goal-kick beat me between my knees;
my goal kick flies into a pram-and-baby.

You eat off your whole-pound chocolate cake;
I swell up halfway to get my mate's help.

My bike hurls me into the hedge;
your bike swerves half-circle from trouble.

I jump the wall and get dumped;
you leap over the wall and laugh, satisfied.

I touch the country bridge and walk;
you talk and talk.

You write poems with line-end rhymes;
I write poems with rhymes nowhere or anywhere.

Your computer game screens monsters and gunners;
my game brings on swimmers and courting red birds.

Postcard Poem: Solo

Mum, you needn't have worried one bit.
I travelled fine, fine, solo. Carried
in steelbird-belly of music shows.
I ate two passengers' pudding twice.
Nibbled nothings nutty and chocolatey.
Sipped cool Cokes. Had more nibbles.
All over mountain after mountain.
Over different oceans. Over
weird clouds, like snow hills
with trails of straggly shapes
drifting, searching. And strangers
talked – Germans going on big-fish hunt,
Italians to ride glass-bottomed boat,
a Dane to do snorkelling. Then, Mum,
I hopped from steelbird-belly, down among
sun-roasted people of a palmtree place.
Welcome to Jamaica, voices called out.
While family hugged a sweating me
and took me off. Other exotics
got collected up in cars and coaches
to be naked on beaches, while
steelbird stood there shiny-ready
for more come-and-go trips.

A Nest Full of Stars

Only chance made me come and find
my hen, stepping from her hidden
nest, in our kitchen garden.

In her clever secret place, her tenth
egg, still warm, had just been dropped.

Not sure of what to do, I picked up
every egg, counting them, then put them
down again. *All were mine.*

All swept me away and back.
I blinked. I saw: a whole hand
of ripe bananas, nesting.

I blinked, I saw: a basketful
of ripe oranges, nesting.

I blinked, I saw: a trayful
of ripe naseberries, nesting.

I blinked, I saw: an open bagful
of ripe mangoes, nesting.

I blinked, I saw:
a mighty nest full of stars.

James Berry

Isn't My Name Magical?

Nobody can see my name on me.
My name is inside
and all over me, unseen
like other people also keep it.
Isn't my name magical?

My name is mine only.
It tells I am individual,
the one special person it shakes
when I'm wanted.

Even if someone else answers
for me, my message hangs in air
haunting others, till it stops
with me, the right name.
Isn't your name and my name magic?

If I'm with hundreds of people
and my name gets called,
my sound switches me on to answer
like it was my human electricity.

My name echoes across playground,
It comes, it demands my attention.
I have to find out who calls,
who wants me for what.
My name gets blurted out in class,
it is terror, at a bad time,
because somebody is cross.

My name gets called in a whisper
I am happy, because
My name may have touched me
with a loving voice.
Isn't your name and my name magic?

Okay, Brown Girl, Okay

for Josie, nine years old, who wrote to me saying, 'Boys
called me names because of my colour. I felt very upset . . .
my brother and sister are English. I wish I was, then I won't
be picked on . . . How do you like being brown?'

Josie, Josie, I am okay
being brown. I remember,
every day dusk and dawn get born
from the loving of night and light
who work together, like married.
    And they would like to say to you:
    Be at school on and on, brown Josie
    like thousands and thousands and thousands
    of children, who are brown and white
    and black and pale-lemon colour.
    All the time, brown girl Josie is okay.

Josie, Josie, I am okay
being brown. I remember,
every minute sun in the sky
and ground of the earth work together
like married.
    And they would like to say to you:
    Ride on up a going escalator
    like thousands and thousands and thousands
    of people, who are brown and white
    and black and pale-lemon colour.
    All the time, brown girl Josie is okay.

Josie, Josie, I am okay
being brown. I remember,
all the time bright-sky and brown-earth
work together, like married
making forests and food and flowers and rain.
    And they would like to say to you:
    Grow and grow brightly, brown girl.
    Write and read and play and work.
    Ride bus or train or boat or aeroplane
    like thousands and thousands and thousands
    of people, who are brown and white
    and black and pale-lemon colour.
    All the time, brown girl Josie is okay.

John Clare

John Clare (1793–1864) worked on farms in Northampton-shire. He also collected local folk songs and wrote poetry. His poems show his love for the countryside. When he was forty-four, he became ill and spent the rest of his life in hospitals, but he kept on writing poetry. Some critics would argue that he was a Romantic poet too, along with others such as Byron and Keats.

I am!

I am! yet what I am none cares or knows,
My friends forsake me like a memory lost;
I am the self-consumer of my woes,
They rise and vanish in oblivious host,
Like shades in love and death's oblivion lost;
And yet I am! and live with shadows tost

Into the nothingness of scorn and noise,
Into the living sea of waking dreams,
Where there is neither sense of life nor joys,
But the vast shipwreck of my life's esteems;
And e'en the dearest – that I loved the best –
Are strange – nay, rather stranger than the rest.

I long for scenes where man has never trod;
A place where woman never smil'd or wept;
There to abide with my creator, God,
And sleep as I in childhood sweetly slept:
Untroubling and untroubled where I lie;
The grass below – above the vaulted sky.

Little Trotty Wagtail

Little trotty wagtail he went in the rain
And tittering tottering sideways he ne'er got straight again
He stooped to get a worm and looked up to catch a fly
And then he flew away ere his feathers they were dry

Little trotty wagtail he waddled in the mud
And left his little foot marks trample where he would
He waddled in the water-pudge and waggle went his tail
And chirrupt up his wings to dry upon the garden rail

Little trotty wagtail you nimble all about
And in the dimpling water-pudge you waddle in and out
Your home is nigh at hand and in the warm pigsty
So little Master Wagtail I'll bid you a 'Good bye'

Evening Schoolboys

Harken that happy shout – the school-house door
Is open thrown and out the yonkers teem
Some run to leapfrog on the rushy moor
And others dabble in the shallow stream
Catching young fish and turning pebbles o'er
For mussel clams – Look at that mellow gleam
Where the retiring sun that rests the while
Streams through the broken hedge – How happy seem
Those schoolboy friendships leaning o'er the stile
Both reading in one book – anon a dream
Rich with new joys doth their young hearts beguile
And the book's pocketed most hastily
Ah happy boys well may ye turn and smile
When joys are yours that never cost a sigh

Haymaking

'Tis haytime and the red-complexioned sun
Was scarcely up ere blackbirds had begun
Along the meadow hedges here and there
To sing loud songs to the sweet-smelling air
Where breath of flowers and grass and happy cow
Fling o'er one's senses streams of fragrance now
While in some pleasant nook the swain and maid
Lean o'er their rakes and loiter in the shade
Or bend a minute o'er the bridge and throw
Crumbs in their leisure to the fish below
– Hark at that happy shout – and song between
'Tis pleasure's birthday in her meadow scene.
What joy seems half so rich from pleasure won
As the loud laugh of maidens in the sun?

Snow Storm

What a night the wind howls hisses and but stops
To howl more loud while the snow volly keeps
Insessant batter at the window pane
Making our comfort feel as sweet again
And in the morning when the tempest drops
At every cottage-door mountainious heaps
Of snow lies drifted that all entrance stops
Untill the beesom and the shovel gains
The path – and leaves a wall on either side –
The shepherd rambling valleys white and wide
With new sensations his old memorys fills
When hedges left at night, no more descried,
Are turned to one white sweep of curving hills
And trees, turned bushes, half their bodys hide

The boy that goes to fodder with surprise
Walks o'er the gate he opened yesternight
The hedges all have vanished from his eyes
E'en some tree tops the sheep could reach to bite
The novel scene emboldens new delight
And though with cautious steps his sports begin
He bolder shuffles the hugh hills of snow
Till down he drops and plunges to the chin
And struggles much and oft escape to win
Then turns and laughs but dare not further go
For deep the grass and bushes lie below
Where little birds that soon at eve went in
With heads tucked in their wings now pine for day
And little feel boys o'er their heads can stray

John Clare

Autumn Morning

The autumn morning waked by many a gun
Throws o'er the fields her many-coloured light
Wood wildly touched close-tanned and stubbles dun
A motley paradise for earth's delight
Clouds ripple as the darkness breaks to light
And clover fields are hid with silver mist
One shower of cobwebs o'er the surface spread
And threads of silk in strange disorder twist
Round every leaf and blossom's bottly head.
Hares in the drowning herbage scarcely steal
But on the battered pathway squats abed
And by the cart-rut nips her morning meal
Look where we may the scene is strange and new
And every object wears a changing hue

Evening

'Tis evening, the black snail has got on his track,
And gone to its nest is the wren;
And the packman-snail too, with his home on his back,
Clings on the bowed bents like a wen.

The shepherd has made a rude mark with his foot
Where his shaddow reached when he first came;
And it just touched the tree where his secret love cut
Two letters that stand for love's name

The evening comes in with the wishes of love
And the shepherd he looks on the flowers
And thinks who would praise the soft song of the dove,
And meet joy in these dewfalling hours

For nature is love, and the wishes of love,
When nothing can hear or intrude;
It hides from the eagle, and joins with the dove
In beautiful green solitude.

James Carter

Eleven things you might not know about James Carter:

JAMES WINSTON HENRY CARTER – what's so funny? – was born 27 November 1959, but can't remember much about it.

ALICE is James's slightly weird but lovable cat – or, more likely, James is Alice's slightly weird but lovable owner.

MUSHROOM OMELETTES, CHEESE AND ONION CRISPS and ICE CREAM – rarely together – are the foods he likes eating most.

ELECTRIC GUITARS have been his lifelong obsession – ever since he heard The Beatles when he was four and he played along with a tennis racket. It took another eleven years for him to save up to buy his first electric guitar. He has been annoying people ever since. People still come up and ask him, 'Whatever happened to that lovely old tennis racket?'

SARAH IS JAMES'S BRILLIANT WIFE and Lauren and Madeleine are his just-as-brilliant daughters. They still buy him tennis rackets and often hide his guitar.

CARS, STARS, ELECTRIC GUITARS (Walker Books) is the name of James's book of poems. The extremely nice puff on the back of the book is from Jacqueline Wilson: 'James Carter is an exciting new voice, imaginative and innovative. Children will love these poems.'

ALWAYS LISTENING TO MUSIC – when driving, washing up or clearing out Alice's cat litter tray – James's favourite music includes David Byrne, Bob Marley and the Wailers, Tom Waits and J. S. Bach.

READING IS a) where he was born and b) something he loves doing very much. (Geddit?)

THINGY, BLUE and APPLE are three of his favourite words. He tries to put them in as many poems as he can.

ENJOYS WRITING POEMS nearly more than anything else – even trainspotting. But James really enjoys all of his work – whether he's teaching adults, writing books for teachers or visiting schools to perform his poems (and play the guitar!) and to do poetry workshops.

RACKET is a) what he makes when he plays the guitar and b) what he played (tennis) before some crazy person sold him the guitar.

Love You More

Do I love you
to the moon and back?
No I love you
more than that

I love you to the desert sands
the mountains, stars
the planets and

I love you to the deepest sea
and deeper still
through history

Before beyond I love you then
I love you now
I'll love you when

The sun's gone out
the moon's gone home
and all the stars are fully grown

When I no longer say these words
I'll give them to the winds, the birds
so that they will still be heard

I love you

Electric Guitars

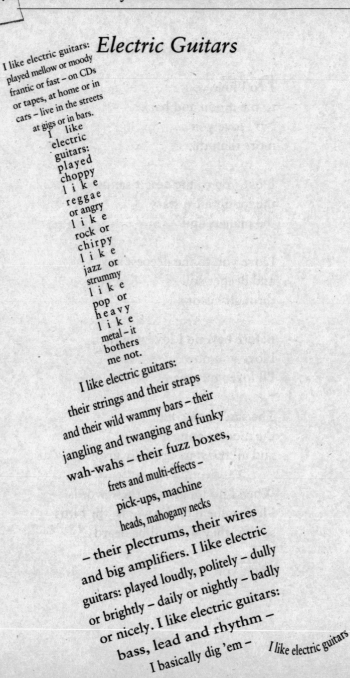

I like electric guitars:
played mellow or moody
frantic or fast – on CDs
or tapes, at home or in
cars – live in the streets
at gigs or in bars.
I   like
electric
guitars:
played
choppy
l i k e
reggae
or angry
l i k e
rock or
chirpy
l i k e
jazz or
strummy
l i k e
pop or
h e a v y
l i k e
metal – it
bothers
me not.

I like electric guitars:
their strings and their straps
and their wild wammy bars – their
jangling and twanging and funky
wah-wahs – their fuzz boxes,
frets and multi-effects –
pick-ups, machine
heads, mahogany necks
– their plectrums, their wires
and big amplifiers. I like electric
guitars: played loudly, politely – dully
or brightly – daily or nightly – badly
or nicely. I like electric guitars:
bass, lead and rhythm –
I basically dig 'em –   I like electric guitars

Take a Poem

Why not take a poem
wherever you go?
pop it in your pocket
nobody will know

Take it to your classroom
stick it on the wall
tell them all about it
read it in the hall

Take it to the bathroom
tuck it up in bed
take the time to learn it
keep it in your head

Take it for a day trip
take it on a train
fold it as a hat
when it starts to rain

Take it to a river
fold it as a boat
pop it in the water
hope that it will float

Take it to a hilltop
fold it as a plane
throw it up skywards
  time and time again

Take it to a post box
send it anywhere
out into the world with
tender
      loving
            care

The Dark

Why are we so afraid of the dark?
It doesn't bite and doesn't bark
Or chase old ladies round the park
Or steal your sweeties for a lark

And though it might not let you see
It lets you have some privacy
And gives you time to go to sleep
Provides a place to hide or weep

It cannot help but be around
When beastly things make beastly sounds
When back doors slam and windows creek
When cats have fights and voices shriek

The dark is cosy, still and calm
And never does you any harm
In the loft, below the sink
It's somewhere nice and quiet to think

Deep in cupboards, pockets too
It's always lurking out of view
Why won't it come out till it's night?
Perhaps the dark's afraid of light

Icy Morning Haiku

On a frozen pond
a small dog is nervously
attempting to skate

Way up in a tree
a black cat grins with delight
watching and waiting

Beneath the clear ice
a big fish wonders if all
dogs walk on water

Inside

Now
you
may think
I'm walking tall
I'm talking big
I've got it all
but here inside
I'm ever so shy
I sometimes cry
I'm curled in a ball
I'm no feet small
no I'm
not big
not tall
at all

Talking Time

Not only the day but also the night
I am the coming and going of light

The growing and turning of shadows on land
the falling of sand, that watch on your hand

The arc of the moon, the tug of the tides
the till of the fields, the sun as it hides

The here and the now and the way back when
in hide-and-seek games: the counting to ten

Your birthday, your last, the lines on your face
the start and the finish of every race

Measure me, treasure me, do as you will
I'll drag or I'll fly but I'll never stay still

If I am your rhythm, then you are my rhyme
we live for each other, and my name is time

Clare Bevan

Clare Bevan lives in a rather dusty house with her husband, Martin, her son, Benedict, one fat, brown hamster called Malteser, and a huge jar of stick insects. Her hobby is acting, and her favourite parts are the funny ones, because she likes to make people laugh. She rides around her village on a wobbly tricycle, and she often dresses up as Rupert when she's collecting money for charity. Where does she get ideas for her poems? In the local coffee shop, or walking around muttering to herself. If she's really stuck, she shuts herself in the garden shed and won't let herself out until she's written something, anything! Her advice to new writers? Carry a notebook EVERYWHERE, so you can capture your best ideas before they escape. And a garden shed can be very useful too.

What does she want to do next? Write a poem that will make a real difference to someone, somewhere. Or just make them laugh.

The Spider

(This poem was pinned to a tiny grave under Clare Bevan's hazel tree.)

The fairy child loved her spider.

Even when it grew fat
And grey and old,
She would comb its warm fur
With a hazel twig
And take it for slow walks
On its silky lead.

Sometimes it played cat-cradles with her
But more often it wove hammocks
Amongst the long grasses
And they swung together under friendly trees.

When it died,
Her mother bought her a money spider
Who scuttled and tumbled to make her smile.
But it wasn't the same,
And still, when she curls up to sleep
In the lonely dawn,
She murmurs her old spider's name.

The Music Lesson Rap

I'm the bongo kid,
I'm the big-drum-beater,
I'm the click-your-sticks,
I'm the tap-your-feeter.
When the lesson starts,
When we clap our hands,
Then it's me who dreams
Of the boom-boom bands,
And it's me who stamps,
And it's me who yells
For the biff-bang gong,
Or the ding-dong bells,
Or the cymbals (large),
Or the cymbals (small),
Or the tubes that chime
Round the bash-crash hall,
Or the tambourine,
Or the thunder-maker –
But all you give me
Is the sssh-sssh shaker!

Clare Bevan

Just Doing My Job

I'm one of Herod's Henchmen
We don't have much to say,
We just charge through the audience
In a Henchman sort of way.

We all wear woolly helmets
To hide our hair and ears,
And Wellingtons sprayed silver
To match our tinfoil spears.

Our swords are made of cardboard
So blood will not be spilled
If we trip and stab a parent
When the hall's completely filled.

We don't look very scary,
We're mostly small and shy,
And some of us wear glasses,
But we give the thing a try.

We whisper Henchman noises
While Herod hunts for strangers,
And then we all charge out again
Like nervous Power Rangers.

Yet when the play is over
And Miss is out of breath
We'll charge like Henchmen through the hall
And scare our mums to death.

Literacy Hour

So let's make this clear,
an ADJECTIVE is a
DESCRIBING word . . .
(The long, winding, deep, dark, gloomy, secret
Tunnel leads under
The cold, bare, windy, wet, empty
Playground to the
Wild, wonderful, sunny, exciting, outside
World.)

And a NOUN, of course,
Is an OBJECT, a SUBJECT,
A THING . . .
(If only I had
A glider, or a private jet, or a space rocket,
   or a hot-air balloon, or a time machine,
I could fly away to
The seaside, or the zoo, or a forest, or Egypt,
   or Disneyland, or Anywhere-But-Here.)

A VERB, as we all know,
I hope,
Is a DOING word . . .
(I could run, or race, or tiptoe, or clamber,
   or catapult, or dance, or whirl, or just walk
My way to freedom.)

And an ADVERB tells you
Exactly how the action
Is done . . .
(Joyfully, happily, noisily, silently, timidly,
   bravely, desperately, frantically, urgently,
       nervously, wistfully, longingly, dreamily,
Someday,
Sometime,
Soon.)

The Blind Dog

My kindly human sighs for me,
But with my clever nose I see . . .

The perfumed path of a lady dog,
The fishy trail of a passing frog,
The sharp, clear stink of a scavenging fox,
The tempting scents of a cardboard box,

The glorious odours of dustbin day,
The tang of a lamp-post in my way,
The feathery whiff of a broken bird,
The traces of ice cream, softly blurred,

The insults left by an old tom cat,
The slimy tracks of a sewer rat,
The homely smell of our garden gate,
The call of the gravy on my plate.

My kindly human sighs for me,
But with my clever nose – I see.

Clare Bevan

The Housemaid's Letter

Dear Mum,
    My life is very fine here
    Far from the village
    And the smells of home.

    I have a room in the roof
    Painted blue as a blackbird's egg,
    And a whole bed to myself,
    Which is lonely
    But so clean
    The sheets crackle like morning frost.

And I have tried
Truly
To make you proud of me, Mum.
I work hard all day,
Cleaning and polishing this great house
Till it sparkles as brightly
As a butterfly's wing.
Then I disappear down the Servants' Stair
Like a small, sweaty,
Fairy Godmother,
Unseen and unknown
By the golden ones above.

And I am happy enough, Mum.
The food is good
Though swallowed in silence.
The other girls smile
At my clumsy ways
And Cook can be kind
If the milk is sweet
And the butter cool.

But sometimes,
When the Sunday bells are ringing,
I still miss the warmth of the little ones
Curled beside me in the tumbled darkness,
And I hunger to hear
The homely peal
Of your lost laughter,
Mum.

Clare Bevan

Letters to the Three Pigs

(Found in a Gingerbread Filing Cabinet, at the 'King Of The Castle' Planning Office.)

Dear Mr Pig, We notice
You've built a house of straw.
You didn't ask permission,
You didn't say what for,
You didn't ring our office,
You didn't write, and so –
Our Big Bad Wolf will be RIGHT ROUND
To huff and puff and blow.

Dear Pig & Co., We're puzzled.
Some creatures never learn.
You've built a house of wooden planks –
The sort that's bound to burn,
The sort that's full of woodworm,
The sort that causes trouble –
Our Big Bad Wolf will be RIGHT ROUND
To smash your place to rubble.

Pig Partners, Now you've done it.
You're either rude or lazy.
You've gone and built a house of bricks
To drive our planners crazy.
You didn't dig foundations,
You knew we'd have to ban it –
Our Big Bad Wolf will be RIGHT ROUND
To blast you off the planet.

Dear Brothers Pig, Our greetings!
We huffed, we puffed, we blew,
We even stormed your chimney,
But NOTHING bothered you –
Our Big Sad Wolf will be RIGHT ROUND
To pay you our respects,
And offer you a splendid job . . .
With Beanstalk Architects.

William Shakespeare

William Shakespeare (1564–1616) was born in Stratford-upon-Avon and moved to London, where he became an actor and writer in the theatre. He is one of the most successful writers ever and his work has remained popular, worldwide, over hundreds of years. He is most well known for his plays, such as *Hamlet*, *Macbeth* and *Romeo and Juliet*. Many of his plays are written in verse, but he also wrote a lot of poems and is famous for writing sonnets. Shakespeare was highly acclaimed by both Queen Elizabeth I and King James I, who allowed him to establish his own theatre company called 'The King's Men', which was very successful. Shakespeare's plays were performed mostly at the Globe Theatre, which, despite being destroyed by a fire in 1613, has recently been rebuilt, and it is now possible to go and see the plays as they would have been performed and seen nearly 400 years ago! Many of his plays have also been made into Hollywood films, such as *Romeo + Juliet*, so his work really does span the ages!

When that I was and a little tiny boy

When that I was and a little tiny boy,
   With hey, ho, the wind and the rain;
A foolish thing was but a toy,
   For the rain it raineth every day.

But when I came to man's estate,
   With hey, ho, the wind and the rain;
'Gainst knaves and thieves men shut their gates,
   For the rain it raineth every day.

But when I came, alas! to wive,
   With hey, ho, the wind and the rain;
By swaggering could I never thrive,
   For the rain it raineth every day.

But when I came unto my beds,
   With hey, ho, the wind and the rain;
With toss-pots still had drunken heads,
   For the rain it raineth every day.

A great while ago the world begun,
   With hey, ho, the wind and the rain;
But that's all one, our play is done,
   And we strive to please you every day.

Fire, Burn; and Cauldron, Bubble

Round about the cauldron go;
In the poison'd entrails throw.
Toad, that under cold stone
Days and nights has thirty-one
Swelter'd venom, sleeping got,
Boil thou first i'th' charmed pot.
Double, double toil and trouble:
Fire, burn; and cauldron, bubble.
Fillet of a fenny snake,
In the cauldron boil and bake;
Eye of newt, and toe of frog,
Wool of bat, and tongue of dog,
Adder's fork, and blind-worm's sting,
Lizard's leg, and howlet's wing.
For a charm of powerful trouble,
Like a hell-broth boil and bubble.
Double, double toil and trouble:
Fire, burn; and cauldron, bubble.

All the world's a stage

All the world's a stage
And all the men and women merely players:
They have their exits and their entrances;
And one man in his time plays many parts,
His acts being seven ages. At first the infant,
Mewling and puking in the nurse's arms.
And then the whining schoolboy, with his satchel,
And shining morning face, creeping like snail
Unwillingly to school. And then the lover,
Sighing like furnace, with a woeful ballad
Made to his mistress' eyebrow. Then a soldier,
Full of strange oaths, and bearded like the pard,
Jealous in honour, sudden and quick in quarrel,
Seeking the bubble reputation
Even in the cannon's mouth. And then the justice,
In fair round belly with good capon lin'd,
With eyes severe, and beard of formal cut,
Full of wise saws and modern instances;
And so he plays his part. The sixth age shifts
Into the lean and slipper'd pantaloon,
With spectacles on nose and pouch on side,
His youthful hose well sav'd, a world too wide
For his shrunk shank; and his big manly voice,
Turning again toward childish treble, pipes
And whistles in his sound. Last scene of all,
That ends this strange eventful history,
Is second childishness and mere oblivion,
Sans teeth, sans eyes, sans taste, sans everything.

William Shakespeare

A Fairy Song

Over hill, over dale,
  Thorough bush, thorough brier,
Over park, over pale,
  Thorough flood, thorough fire!
I do wander everywhere,
Swifter than the moon's sphere;
And I serve the fairy queen,
To dew her orbs upon the green;
The cowslips tall her pensioners be;
In their gold coats spots you see;
Those be rubies, fairy favours,
In those freckles live their savours:
I must go seek some dewdrops here,
And hang a pearl in every cowslip's ear.

Sonnet 18

Shall I compare thee to a summer's day?
Thou art more lovely and more temperate:
Rough winds do shake the darling buds of May,
And summer's lease hath all too short a date:
Sometime too hot the eye of heaven shines,
And often is his gold complexion dimm'd;
And every fair from fair sometime declines,
By chance or nature's changing course untrimm'd;
But thy eternal summer shall not fade,
Nor lose possession of that fair thou ow'st;
Nor shall Death brag thou wander'st in his shade,
When in eternal lines to time thou grow'st:
   So long as men can breathe, or eyes can see,
   So long lives this, and this gives life to thee.

Ariel's Song

Full fathom five thy father lies,
Of his bones are coral made:
Those are pearls that were his eyes,
Nothing of him that doth fade,
But doth suffer a sea-change
Into something rich, and strange:
Sea-nymphs hourly ring his knell –
  Hark! now I hear them,
    Ding-dong bell.

Where the Bee Sucks

Where the bee sucks, there suck I:
In a cowslip's bell I lie;
There I couch when owls do cry.
On the bat's back I do fly
After summer merrily.
Merrily, merrily shall I live now
Under the blossom that hangs on the bough.

Nick Toczek

Nick Toczek was born in Bradford in 1950 and still lives there. He's married with two teenage children who like to spend his money. He breeds lizards (bearded dragons) and writes every day, for adults as well as for children. He's published about three dozen books, mostly of poetry, but also novels, short story collections, a pantomime, a musical and some non-fiction too. He's also a professional magician, puppeteer, stand-up comedian and journalist. This means that he gets to do most of his hobbies for a living. How lucky is that? He tours throughout Britain doing one-man shows for children, for families or just for adults and has also performed throughout Europe, in Canada, America and even in China. For more information on Nick, try doing an Internet search. Just put his name into a search engine such as Google and you'll find hundreds of sites that'll tell you more about him.

Staff Meeting

The teachers have gathered in private to talk
About their collections of leftover chalk –
Bits that are rare, bits they just like,
And fragments they've saved just in case there's a strike.
One has a blue that you don't often see,
Another a remnant from nineteen-oh-three.

They've thousands of pieces in boxes and tins,
Each sorted and counted with tweezers and pins.
And when all their best bits have been on display,
They'll take them home carefully, and lock them away.

The End of School

We shove gloves and scarves on.
It's shivery and stark.
And out in the playground
It's evening and dark.
We rattle the railings
With sticks for a lark.

The sky's grown as grey
As the skin of a shark.
The branches are bare
On the trees in the park.
The wind took their leaves
Leaving winter-proof bark.

The streetlights are waking
And making their mark.
At first they're a dull red
And glow like a spark,
Grow orange, then yellow –
A dazzling arc.

'They're forecasting snow,'
I heard one mum remark.
Sleet comes, then the bus comes.
We loudly embark.
The sunshine of summer's
Fled south like the lark.

The Great Escape

In the Great Escape from London Zoo
eight caribou and gnu they knew
mounted a minor military coup,
an act of animal derring-do,
and locked the staff they overthrew
in the 'potamus pit and a portaloo,
then caught a plane to North Peru.

As animals broke out two-by-two
to squeal and growl and grunt and moo
a loud unruly queue soon grew
that wriggled and ran and crawled and flew,
stampeding down the avenue.

In the Great Escape from London Zoo
we heard how a herd of kangaroo
had bid the big brown owl adieu
with a: 'Toodle-oo, mate, toodle-oo!'
but before he'd time to twit-tu-woo
they'd hopped it, heading for Timbuktu
and the owl himself had flown off too.

While a crocodile and a cockatoo
crossed the Thames in a slim canoe,
rowed by the bird, so the croc could chew . . .
chew through the bones of the eight-man crew
till the river ran red instead of blue.

In the Great Escape from London Zoo
the pandas abandoned their bamboo
and, all dressed up as railway crew,
hijacked the fifteen fifty-two
from platform three at Waterloo
and 'parley-voo' they zoomed straight through
Paris, and on to Katmandu.

Panic ensued and ballyhoo
when pot-bellied pig and rare-breed ewe
gatecrashed a very posh barbecue
terribly upsetting the well-to-do
and causing a heck of a hullabaloo.

You doubt my word? What's wrong with you?
Why, every detail here is true.
The Great Escape from London Zoo.
When was that? I thought you knew:
Years ago, at half-past two.

Victorian Diarist

My name is Ebenezer Grey.
I wear my top hat every day,
but take it off to go to bed
and put my nightcap on instead.
Before I sleep I always write,
in Indian ink by candlelight,
neat notes nibbed in copperplate
on what I've known and done that date.

It's the diary of Ebenezer Grey
who wore his top hat all that day
and, though each day is much the same,
he fills its page, then snuffs the flame.
And downstairs in the darkened hall,
the tall clock stands, with back to wall.
It ticks and tuts, solemnly dour,
and all night chimes to mark the hour.

Undreaming, Ebenezer Grey,
who'll wear his top hat all today,
is roused by maid with morning meal.
Outside the sounds of hoof and wheel.
Now nearer noises fill his room
of shovelled coal and driven broom;
while waking smells of baking bread
give way to polish, soaps, blacklead.

Good morning, Ebenezer Grey!
Your top hat's there again today.
You're trimmed and tailored, looking fine,
stiff collar upright, like your spine.
You've breakfasted on bread and kippers.
You've read *The Times* in gown and slippers.
Now groomed and dressed with waxed moustache
you're dapper, without being flash.

Yes, I am Ebenezer Grey.
I wear this top hat every day.
I pause to raise it when I meet
an old acquaintance in the street.
We nod and smile to be polite
though conversation wouldn't be right.
Besides, I very seldom speak
save once or maybe twice a week.

So there goes Ebenezer Grey,
top-hatted for another day.
Across the park with walking cane
he strides to horse-drawn tram or train.
At five-fifteen, he's home again,
his life a pattern he'll maintain
till death comes knocking on his door
in the spring of 1894.

Saturday Evening

From Dundee to Dover
The games are all over
And those who have lost
Will be counting the cost . . .

I know it'll vex 'em
In Oldham and Wrexham.
At Clydebank and Clyde
They'll have cried and have cried.
They'll be glumly pathetic
At Charlton Athletic,
But moodily manly
At Accrington Stanley.

Cos nobody likes to lose.
They stand there and stare at their shoes.
They're gob-smacked and gutted
Like they've been head-butted.
Life's not worth a carrot.
They're sick as a parrot
And struggle to cope with the news.

At Manchester City
They're full of self-pity.
At Port Vale they're pale,
At Alloa, sallower,
Sullen in Fulham.
Morose at Montrose,
And Bradford and Burnley
Just sulk taciturnly.

Cos nobody likes to lose.
They stand there and stare at their shoes.
They're gob-smacked and gutted
Like they've been head-butted.
Life's not worth a carrot.
They're sick as a parrot
And struggle to cope with the news.

And down Grimsby Town
Oh, how grimly they frown!
And Partick and Chelsea
Grow sick and unhealthy,
While at Aston Villa
They're very much iller,
And it's really killing 'em
In Millwall and Gillingham.

Cos nobody likes to lose.
They stand there and stare at their shoes.
They're gob-smacked and gutted
Like they've been head-butted.
Life's not worth a carrot.
They're sick as a parrot
And struggle to cope with the news.

In Barnsley and Barnet
They spit and say, 'Darn it!'
At Preston North End
Now they're nobody's friend.
And down Crystal Palace
They bristle with malice,
While Reading and Rangers
Are dangers to strangers.

Cos nobody likes to lose.
They stand there and stare at their shoes.
They're gob-smacked and gutted
Like they've been head-butted.
Life's not worth a carrot.
They're sick as a parrot
And struggle to cope with the news.

Some fans of Southend
Have just gone round the bend,
And they're less than delighted
At West Ham United.
And down-in-the-mouth
Up in Queen of the South
While they look like leftovers
At poor Tranmere Rovers.

Cos nobody likes to lose.
They stand there and stare at their shoes.
They're gob-smacked and gutted
Like they've been head-butted.
Life's not worth a carrot.
They're sick as a parrot
And struggle to cope with the news.

Not a grin or a smile
Around Plymouth Argyle,
While they fret and they frown
Down in Kettering Town.
They're crestfallen and pale
In Walsall and Rochdale,
And it's gone past a joke
For Doncaster and Stoke.

Cos nobody likes to lose.
They stand there and stare at their shoes.
They're gob-smacked and gutted
Like they've been head-butted.
Life's not worth a carrot.
They're sick as a parrot
And struggle to cope with the news.

In York and Hull City
The talk isn't pretty,
While Torquay and Lincoln
Have taken to drinkin'.
You'll not find a jester
In Chester or Leicester –
They've got lots to bother 'em
And so've Notts and Rotherham.

Cos nobody likes to lose.
They stand there and stare at their shoes.
They're gob-smacked and gutted
Like they've been head-butted.
Life's not worth a carrot.
They're sick as a parrot
And struggle to cope with the news.

They're not very merry
In Blackburn and Bury.
They're choking in Woking
Where no one is joking.
There's an air of despair
In the air over Ayr,
And the black cloud's a big 'un
That hangs over Wigan.

Cos nobody likes to lose.
They stand there and stare at their shoes.
They're gob-smacked and gutted
Like they've been head-butted.
Life's not worth a carrot.
They're sick as a parrot
And struggle to cope with the news.

Seasick

'I don't feel welk,' whaled the squid, sole-fully.
'What's up?' asked the doctopus.
'I've got sore mussels and a tunny-hake,' she told him.

'Lie down and I'll egg salmon you,' mermaid the doctopus.
'Rays your voice,' said the squid. 'I'm a bit hard of herring.'
'Sorry! I didn't do it on porpoise,' replied the doctopus orc-
wardly.

He helped her to oyster self on to his couch
And asked her to look up so he could sea urchin.
He soon flounder plaice that hurt.

'This'll make it eel,' he said, whiting a prescription.
'So I won't need to see the sturgeon?' she asked.
'Oh, no,' he told her. 'In a couple of dace you'll feel brill.'

'Cod bless you,' she said.
'That'll be sick squid,' replied the doctopus.

Nick Toczek

The Dragon Who Ate Our School

1

The day the dragon came to call,
she ate the gate, the playground wall
and, slate by slate, the roof and all,
the staffroom, gym and entrance hall,
and every classroom, big or small.

So . . .
She's undeniably great.
She's absolutely cool,
the dragon who ate
the dragon who ate
the dragon who ate our school.

2

Pupils panicked. Teachers ran.
She flew at them with wide wingspan.
She slew a few and then began
to chew through the lollipop man,
two parked cars and a transit van.

Wow . . . !
She's undeniably great.
She's absolutely cool,
the dragon who ate
the dragon who ate
the dragon who ate our school.

Nick Toczek

3
She bit off the head of the head.
She said she was sad he was dead.
He bled and he bled and he bled.
And as she fed, her chin went red
and then she swallowed the cycle shed.

Oh . . .
She's undeniably great.
She's absolutely cool,
the dragon who ate
the dragon who ate
the dragon who ate our school.

4
It's thanks to her that we've been freed.
We needn't write. We needn't read.
Me and my mates are all agreed,
we're very pleased with her indeed.
So clear the way, let her proceed.

Cos . . .
She's undeniably great.
She's absolutely cool,
the dragon who ate
the dragon who ate
the dragon who ate our school.

5

There was some stuff she couldn't eat.
A monster forced to face defeat,
she spat it out along the street –
the dinner ladies' veg and meat
and that pink muck they serve for sweet.

But . . .
She's undeniably great.
She's absolutely cool,
the dragon who ate
the dragon who ate
the dragon who ate our school.

Gareth Owen

Gareth Owen says: 'As a lad in Ainsdale, Lancashire, it never crossed my mind to be a writer. I had seen writers in films; they smoked pipes, drove snazzy cars and were brave in the war. My dream was to play midfield for Everton. At school, being pretty awful at everything except English and football, I left at sixteen to join the Merchant Navy. One clear, blue day in Buenos Aires, I fell from a rope on to the deck, sustaining a triple fracture. Not good for the brain! So, I became an English and drama teacher in Ilford. Looking through the school anthologies, I couldn't find a single poem about everyday life. One day I heard the voice of a Lancashire schoolboy in my head, and made what he was telling me into a poem which I called 'Our School'. I wrote others like it and they ended up in a book called *Salford Road*. I then started lecturing in a training college in Birmingham, supervising students teaching English. While there, I started acting, and writing novels and plays. I also met the soul singer Ruby Turner and ended up managing her and running an independent record company. For a time, I also presented the BBC's *Verse Universe* and *Poetry Please*. I have since retired to Ludlow and retirement is the best job I've ever had. More books? I hope so. Watch this space.'

Gareth Owen

Our School

I go to Weld Park Primary,
it's near the Underpass
And five blocks past the Cemetery
And two roads past the Gas
Works with the big tower that smells so bad
   me and me mates put our hankies over our
      faces and pretend we're being attacked
         by poison gas . . . and that.

There's this playground with lines for rounders,
And cricket stumps chalked on the wall,
And kids with their coats for goalposts
Booting a tennis ball
Around all over the place and shoutin' and arguin'
   about offside and they always kick it over
      the garden wall next door and she
         goes potty and tells our head teacher
         and he gets right ratty with
           everybody and stops us playin'
           football . . .
            . . . and everything.

We have this rule at our school
You've to wait till the whistle blows
And you can't go in till you hear it
Not even if it snows.
And your wellies get filled with water and your socks
   go all soggy and start slipping down your legs
     and your hands get so cold they go all
        crumpled and you can't undo
          the buttons of your mac when
            you do get inside . . .
              . . . it's true.

The best thing is our classroom.
When it's fine you can see right far,
Past the Catholic Cathedral
Right to the Morris Car
Works where me dad works as a fitter and sets off
   right early every morning in these overalls
     with his snap in this sandwich box and
        a flask of tea and always moanin'
          about the money . . . honest.

In Hall we pray for brotherly love
And sing hymns that are ever so long
And the Head shouts at Linda Nutter
Who's always doing wrong.
She can't keep out of trouble because
  she's always talkin'
    she can't stop our teacher says she
      must have been injected with
        a gramophone needle she talks
        so much and
that made me laugh once
not any more though I've heard it
too often . . . teachers!

Loving your enemy sounds all right
Until you open your eyes
And you're standing next to Nolan
Who's always telling lies
About me and getting me into trouble and about
  three times a week I fight him after school
    it's a habit I've got
      but I can't love him even though
        I screw my eyes up real hard and try like
        mad, but if it wasn't him it
        would be somebody else
        I mean
          you've got to have enemies . . .
          . . . haven't you?

We sing 'O to be a pilgrim'
And think about God and heaven
And then we're told the football team lost
By thirteen goals to seven
But that's not bad because St Xavier's don't half have
     big lads in their team and last time we played
          they beat us eighteen one and this time
               we got seven goals . . .
                    . . . didn't we?

Then we have our lessons,
We have Science and English and Maths,
Except on Wednesday morning
When our class goes to the baths
And it's not half cold and Peter Bradberry's
     fingers went all wrinkled and blue last week
          and I said, 'You're goin' to die, man'
               but he pushed me under the water and I had to
               hold my breath for fifteen minutes.
                    But he's still alive though . . .
                         . . . he is.

Friday's my favourite day though,
We have Art all afternoon
And I never care what happens
Cos I know it's home-time soon
And I'm free for two whole days but I think
   sometimes it wouldn't be half so good
      having this weekend if we didn't have five
       days
         of
           school
             in
                between –
Would it?

Tuesday

Denis Law

I live at 14 Stanhope Street,
Me mum, me dad and me,
And three of us have made a gang,
John Stokes and Trev and me.

Our favourite day is Saturday;
We go Old Trafford way
And wear red colours in our coats
To watch United play.

We always stand behind the goal
In the middle of the roar.
The others come to see the game –
I come for Denis Law.

His red sleeves flap around his wrists,
He's built all thin and raw,
But the toughest backs don't stand a chance
When the ball's near Denis Law.

He's a whiplash when he's in control,
He can swivel like an eel,
And twist and sprint in such a way
It makes defences reel.

And when he's hurtling for the goal
I know he's got to score.
Defences may stop normal men –
They can't stop Denis Law.

We all race home when full time blows
To kick a tennis ball,
And Trafford Park is our backyard,
And the stand is next door's wall.

Old Stokesey shouts, 'I'm Jimmy Greaves,'
And scores against the door,
And Trev shouts: 'I'll be Charlton,' –
But I am Denis Law.

Den to Let

To let
One self-contained
Detached den.
Accommodation is compact
Measuring one yard square.
Ideal for two eight-year-olds
Plus one small dog
Or two cats
Or six gerbils.
Accommodation consists of:
One living room
Which doubles as kitchen
Bedroom
Entrance-hall
Dining room
Dungeon
Space capsule
Pirate boat
Covered wagon
Racing car
Palace
Aeroplane
Junk-room
And lookout post.
Property is southward facing
And can be found
Within a short walking distance
Of the back door

At bottom of garden.
Easily found in the dark
By following the smell
Of old cabbages and tea bags
Convenient escape routes
Past rubbish dump
To Seager's Lane
Through hole in hedge,
Or into next door's garden;
But beware of next door's rhinoceros
Who sometimes thinks he's a poodle.
Construction is of
Sound corrugated iron
And roof doubles as shower
During rainy weather.
Being partially underground,
Den makes
A particularly effective hiding place
When in a state of war
With older sisters
Brothers
Angry neighbours
Or when you simply want to be alone.
Some repair work needed
To north wall
Where Mr Spence's foot came through
When planting turnips last Thursday.
With den go all contents
Including:
One carpet – very smelly

One teapot – cracked
One woolly penguin –
No beak and only one wing
One unopened tin
Of sultana pud
One hundred and three *Beano*s
Dated 1983–1985
And four *Rupert* annuals.
Rent is free
The only payment being
That the new occupant
Should care for the den
In the manner to which it has been accustomed
And on long summer evenings
Heroic songs of days gone by
Should be loudly sung
So that old and glorious days
Will never be forgotten.

Conversation Piece

Late again Blenkinsop?
What's the excuse this time?
Not my fault sir.
Whose fault is it then?
Grandma's sir.
Grandma's. What did she do?
She died sir.
Died?
She's seriously dead all right sir.
That makes four grandmothers this term
And all on PE days Blenkinsop.
I know. It's very upsetting sir.
How many grandmothers have you got Blenkinsop?
Grandmothers sir? None sir.
None?
All dead sir.
And what about yesterday Blenkinsop?
What about yesterday sir?
You missed maths.
That was the dentist sir.
The dentist died?
No sir. My teeth sir.
You missed the test Blenkinsop.
I'd been looking forward to it too sir.
Right, line up for PE.
Can't sir.
No such word as can't. Why can't you?
No kit sir.

Where is it?
Home sir.
What's it doing at home?
Not ironed sir.
Couldn't you iron it?
Can't do it sir.
Why not?
My hand sir.
Who usually does it?
Grandma sir.
Why couldn't she do it?
Dead sir.

Typewriting Class

Dear Miss Hinson
I am spitting
In front of my top ratter
With the rest of my commercesnail sturdy students
Triping you this later.
The truce is Miss Hinson
I am not hippy wiht my cross.
Every day on Woundsday
I sit in my dusk
With my type rutter
Trooping without lurking at the lattice
All sorts of weird messengers.
To give one exam pill,
'The quick down socks . . .
The quick brine pox . . .
The sick frown box . . .
The sick down jocks
Humps over the hazy bog'
When everyone knows
That a sick down jock
Would not be seen dead
Near a hazy bog.
Another one we tripe is:
'Now is the tame
For all guide men
To cram to the head
Of the pratty.'
To may why of sinking

If that is all you get to tripe
In true whelks of sturdy
Then I am thinking of changing
To crookery crasses.
I would sooner end up a crook
Than a shirt hand trappist
Any die of the wink.
I have taken the tremble, Miss Hinson
To tripe you this later
So that you will be able
To underhand my indignation
I must clothe now
As the Bill is groaning
                              Yours fitfully . . .

Miss Creedle Teaches Creative Writing

'This morning,' cries Miss Creedle,
'We're all going to use our imaginations,
We're going to close our eyes 3W and imagine.
Are we ready to imagine, Darren?
I'm going to count to three.
At one, we wipe our brains completely clean;
At two, we close our eyes;
And at three, we imagine.
Are we all imagining? Good.
Here is a piece of music by Beethoven to help us.
Beethoven's dates were 1770 to 1827.
(See The Age of Revolutions in your History books.)
Although Beethoven was deaf and a German
He wrote many wonderful symphonies,
But this was a long time before anyone of us was born.
Are you imagining a time before you were born?
What does it look like? Is it dark?
(Embryo is a good word you might use.)
Does the music carry you away like a river?
What is the name of the river? Can you smell it?
Foetid is an exciting adjective.
As you float down the river
Perhaps you land on an alien planet.
Tell me what sounds you hear.
If there are indescribable monsters
Tell me what they look like but not now.
(Your book entitled *Tackle Pre-History This Way*
Will be of assistance here.)
Perhaps you are cast adrift in a broken barrel

In stormy shark-infested waters
(Remember the work we did on piranhas for RE?)
Try to see yourself. Can you do that?
See yourself at the bottom of a pothole in the Andes
With both legs broken
And your life ebbing away inexorably.
What does the limestone feel like?
See the colours.
Have you done that? Good.
And now you may open your eyes.
Your imagining time is over,
Now it is writing time.
Are we ready to write? Good.
Then write away.
Wayne, you're getting some exciting ideas down.
Tracy, that's lovely.
Darren, you haven't written anything.
Couldn't you put the date?
You can't think of anything to write.
Well, what did you see when you closed your eyes?
But you must have seen something beside the black.
Yes, apart from the little squiggles.
Just the black. I see.
Well, try to think
Of as many words for black as you can.'

Miss Creedle whirls about the class
Like a benign typhoon
Spinning from one quailing homestead to another.
I dream of peaceful ancient days
In Mr Swindell's class
When the hours passed like a dream
Filled with order and measuring and tests.
Excitement is not one of the things I come to school for.
I force my eyes shut
But all I see
Is a boy of twelve
Sitting at a desk one dark November day
Writing this poem
And Darren is happy to discover
There is only one word for black
And that will have to suffice
Until the bell rings for all of us.

The Commentator

Good afternoon and welcome
To this international
Between England and Holland
Which is being played here today
At 4, Florence Terrace.
And the pitch looks in superb condition
As Danny Markey, the England captain,
Puts England on the attack.
Straight away it's Markey
With a lovely little pass to Keegan,
Keegan back to Markey,
Markey in possession here
Jinking skilfully past the dustbins;
And a neat flick inside the cat there.
What a brilliant player this Markey is
And he's still only nine years old!
Markey to Francis,
Francis back to Markey,
Markey is through, he's through,
No, he's been tackled by the drainpipe;
But he's won the ball back brilliantly
And he's advancing on the Dutch keeper,
It must be a goal.
The keeper's off his line
But Markey chips him superbly
And it's a goal
No!
It's gone into Mrs Spence's next door.

And Markey's going round to ask for his ball back,
It could be the end of this international.
Now the door's opening
And yes, it's Mrs Spence,
Mrs Spence has come to the door.
Wait a minute
She's shaking her head, she is shaking her head,
She's not going to let England have their ball back.
What is the referee going to do?
Markey's coming back looking very dejected,
And he seems to be waiting . . .
He's going back,
Markey is going back for that ball!
What a brilliant and exciting move!
He waited until the front door was closed
And then went back for that ball.
And wait a minute,
He's found it, Markey has found that ball,
He has found that ball
And that's wonderful news
For the hundred thousand fans gathered here
Who are showing their appreciation
In no uncertain fashion.
But wait a minute,
The door's opening once more.
It's her, it's Mrs Spence
And she's waving her fist
And shouting something I can't quite understand
But I don't think it's encouragement.
And Markey's off,
He's jinked past her on the outside

Dodging this way and that
With Mrs Spence in hot pursuit.
And he's past her, he's through,
What skills this boy has!
But Mr Spence is there too,
Mr Spence in the sweeper role
With Rover their dog.
Markey's going to have to pull out all the stops now.
He's running straight at him,
And he's down, he's down on all fours!
What is he doing?
And Oh my goodness that was brilliant,
That was absolutely brilliant,
He's dived through Spence's legs;
But he's got him,
This rugged stopper has him by the coat
And Rover's barking in there too;
He'll never get out of this one.
But this is unbelievable!
He's got away
He has got away:
He wriggled out of his coat
And left part of his trousers with Rover.
This boy is real dynamite.
He's over the wall
He's clear
They'll never catch him now.
He's down the yard and on his way
And I don't think we're going to see
Any more of Markey
Until it's safe to come home.

David Harmer

David Harmer was born in 1952. For many years he was a primary-school head teacher in Doncaster, where he lives with his wife, Paula. They have two grown-up daughters, Lizzie and Harriet, five cats, two lizards, a dog and three fish.

These days, David works full-time as a writer and performer in schools. He has many poems and stories published in many different books, but mostly his work is published by Macmillan Children's Books, including a book of his own work and several he's edited. He has appeared numerous times on radio and television and performs in the popular poetry duo *Spill The Beans* with his friend Paul Cookson. He has an MA in Writing Studies from Sheffield Hallam University.

David Harmer

South to North; 1965

I was born south of the river
down in the delta, beyond the bayou
lived in the swamps just off the High Street
London alligators snapping my ankles.

It was Bromley, Beckenham, Penge, Crystal Palace
where the kids said *wotcha*, ate bits of *cike*,
the land my father walked as a boy
the land his father walked before him.

I was rooted there, stuck in the clay
until we drove north, moved to Yorkshire
a land of cobbles, coal pits and coke works
forges and steel, fires in the sky.

Where you walked through fields around your village
didn't need three bus-rides to see a farm.

It was Mexbrough, Barnsley, Sprotbrough, Goldthorpe
I was deafened by words, my tongue struck dumb
gobsmacked by a language I couldn't speak in.

Ayop, sithee, it's semmers nowt
What's tha got in thi snap, chaze else paze?
Who does tha support, Owls else Blades?
Dun't thee tha me, thee tha thi sen
Tha's a rate 'un thee, giz a spice?

Cheese and peas, sweets and football
I rolled in a richness of newfound vowels
words that dazed, dazzled and danced
out loud in my head until it all made sense
in this different country, far away
from where I was born, south of the river.

Tuesday

Mister Moore

Mister Moore, Mister Moore
Creaking down the corridor.

Uh uh eh eh uh
Uh uh eh eh uh

Mister Moore wears wooden suits
Mister Moore's got great big boots
Mister Moore's got hair like a brush
And Mister Moore don't like me much.

Mister Moore, Mister Moore
Creaking down the corridor.

Uh uh eh eh uh
Uh uh eh eh uh

David Harmer

When my teacher's there I haven't got a care
I can do my sums, I can do gerzinters
When Mister Moore comes through the door
Got a wooden head filled with splinters.

Mister Moore, Mister Moore
Creaking down the corridor.

Uh uh eh eh uh
Uh uh eh eh uh

Mister Moore I implore
My earholes ache, my head is sore
Don't come through that classroom door
Don't come through that classroom door.
Mister Mister Mister Moore
He's creaking down the corridor.

Uh uh eh eh uh
Uh uh eh eh uh

Big voice big hands
Big voice he's a very big man
Take my advice, be good be very very nice
Be good be very very nice
To Mister Moore, Mister Moore
Creaking down the corridor

Uh uh eh eh uh
Uh uh eh eh uh

Mister Moore wears wooden suits
Mister Moore's got great big boots
Mister Moore's got his hair like a brush
Mister Moore don't like me much

Mister Moore, Mister Moore
Creaking down the corridor.

Uh uh eh eh uh
Uh uh eh eh uh

One Moment in Summer

The house is dropping swallows
one by one from under the gutter

they swoop and fall
on our heads as we queue
for ice cream.

It is so hot
that the long line of cars clogging the road
hums like a line of electric fires.

They shine and shimmer, stink of oil and warm seats
the children gaze out from their misted windows.

Trapped under glass
hair plastered down with sweat
gasping for breath like frogs under ice.

The cars crawl round the curve
of the road, stuck in between the shop
and the cafe.

My ice cream is butterscotch and almond
Lizzie's is chocolate, Harriet's vanilla.

They are so delicious and cold
we lick them slowly, letting the long, cool flavours
slide down our tongues.

Inside the cars, the red-faced people
begin to boil.

The swallows flit and dart
rapid specks of blueblack and white
the summer flies at us
like an arrow.

Sir Guy Is In His Keep Tonight

The twelfth of December 1231
terrible snows, darkness, no sun
the castle is cold, silent and grey
I'm here on my own
my wife and children far away
on a winter holiday.
I've spent all the morning jousting
knocking knights off their horses
then archery in the butts, some swordplay
but I'm on my own tonight, of course
I've got all my servants and soldiers
the fires burning bright
but I'm alone in the keep
on my own
tonight.

I can see them clearly
swarming over the curtain wall
flooding the inner bailey
the thousand ghosts of the thousand Saxons
my father and his father
slaughtered daily
the Saxons fought well, died hard
look at them cover the castle's yard
ghosts, grey in the moonlight
bearded warriors of yesterday
coming for me
tonight.

David Harmer

Dobbo's First Swimming Lesson

Dobbo's fists
spiked me to the playground wall
nailed me to the railings.

The plastic ball
he kicked against my skinny legs
on winter playtimes

Bounced a stinging red-hot bruise
across the icy tarmac.

The day we started swimming
we all jumped in
laughed and splashed, sank beneath
the funny tasting water.

Shivering in a corner
Dobbo crouched, stuck to the side,
sobbing like my baby brother
when all the lights go out.

At Cider Mill Farm

I remember my uncle's farm
Still in mid-summer
Heat hazing the air above the red roof tops
Some cattle sheds, a couple of stables
Clustered round a small yard
Lying under the hills that stretched their long back
Through three counties.

I rolled with his dogs
Among the hay bales
Stacked high in the barn he built himself
During a storm one autumn evening
Tunnelled for treasure or jumped with a scream
From a pirate ship's mast into the straw
Burrowed for gold and found he'd buried
Three battered Ford cars deep in the hay.

He drove an old tractor that sweated oil
In long black streaks down the rusty orange
It chugged and whirred; coughed into life
Each day as he clattered across the cattle grids
I remember one night my cousin and I
Dragging back cows from over the common
We prodded the giant steaming flanks
Pushed them homeward through the rain
And then drank tea from huge tin mugs
Feeling like farmers.

He's gone now, he sold it
But I have been back for one last look
To the twist in the lane that borders the stream
Where Mary, Ruth and I once waded
Water sloshing over our wellies
And I showed my own children my uncle's farm,
The barn still leaning over the straw,
With for all I know three battered Ford cars
Still buried beneath it.

Sunday

Playing Tennis with Justin

It's dinnertime and very sunny
I'm on the yard playing tennis with Justin.
Justin is winning fifty-five nil.

He's got a proper tennis bat called a rocket
I haven't got one so he gave me his spare one.
His rocket is filled up with string, mine isn't
Mine's got lots of holes.

If I hit the ball with the bit with no holes
It goes quite a long way, but usually
Justin says I've hit the net.

We haven't got a net but Justin says
He knows where it would be
If we did have one.
Justin's very clever like that.

He's just scored fifteen more points
I nearly scored one a moment ago
But Justin said it was offside.
So the score is seventy-nil to him.

Justin says that my score is called love
Not nil, well I don't love it much
I keep losing, Justin says not to worry
I might score a six in a minute.

He says it's his second serve for juice
Well, the dinner lady hasn't called our group
In yet, so I haven't had one serving or any juice
I'm starving and it's very hot.

Justin says he's scored three more goals
and I should keep my eye on the ball
Then I might hit it with my rocket.

If Justin doesn't shut up quick
I might hit him with my rocket
I think tennis is rubbish.

Justin says we can play at cricket if I want
But I've got to go in goals
Sometimes you just can't win
With Justin.

Valerie Bloom

Valerie Bloom was born in Orange Hill, Jamaica, grew up in the nearby town of Frankfield, and came to England in 1979. She studied English with African and Caribbean Studies at the University of Kent at Canterbury from 1982–84. In 1995 the same university awarded her an Honorary Masters Degree for her work as a poet.

Valerie has performed her poetry extensively throughout Britain and the Caribbean. She has run writing courses for the Arvon Foundation, in-service courses for teachers and librarians, and writing workshops in schools and colleges.

Valerie is a prolific writer who has been published in over 200 adult and children's anthologies. Her poems have been featured in Poems on the Underground and the *Independent*.

Valerie has been a librarian, a teacher, a steel-band instructor and an arts officer. She now writes, performs and conducts workshops full-time.

Valerie Bloom

Pinda Cake

De pinda cake lady comin' down,
With her basket an' glass case she comin' to town,
She stop by the school gate an' set up her stall,
An' while she a-set up hear de old lady bawl:

Pinda! Pinda cake!
Pinda! Pinda cake!
Gal an' bwoy me jus' done bake,
Come buy yuh lovely pinda cake!

She have grater cake an' she have duckunoo'
Coconut drops an' bulla cake too,
Jackass corn an' plantain tart,
But the t'ing dat dearest to me heart

Is *Pinda! Pinda cake!*
Pinda! Pinda cake!
Gal an' bwoy me jus' done bake,
Come buy yuh lovely pinda cake!

We all crowd round her an' yuh can tell
By de look o' de cake dem, an' de spicy smell
Dat they won't stay in de glass case too long,
As we buy from de lady, we join in the song.

Pinda! Pinda cake!
Pinda! Pinda cake!
Gal an' bwoy me jus' done bake,
Come buy yuh lovely pinda cake!

How to Ask for a Hamster

Mum, can I keep a snake in my room?
What did you say? Are you mad?
Well, Jamie keeps a snake in *his* room,
He got it from his dad.

Will you buy me a mongoose, Mum?
I've played with one; it belongs to Maria,
It's really docile; can I please, Mum?
I don't think that's a good idea!

Can I have a pony then?
I could afford to pay for hay.
D'you know how much a pony costs?
Japhet got one for *his* birthday.

How about a crocodile?
They sell them in Didcot,
I think that's where Chloe bought hers.
Can I have one? *Cetainly not!*

I'll settle for a tarantula then,
It would be in a cage, of course.
Joshua has a tarantula.
Oh no! I can think of nothing worse!

What about a little monkey?
Tina has a chimpanzee.
Everyone in class has a pet,
Everybody except me.

You can have a cat or a hamster,
You cannot have a snake or a mouse.
No crocs, monkey or creepy-crawlies,
I won't have a zoo in this house.

OK, I'll settle for a hamster,
It's better than nothing, I suppose.
Oh, there's the bell, must be Jamie,
We promised to go and play at Joe's.

Jamie, you were right, I tried it,
Just like you said, it worked a treat,
I'm getting the hamster, now tell me
How do I ask for a parakeet?

Frost

Overnight, a giant spilt icing sugar on the ground,
He spilt it on the hedgerows, and the trees without
a sound,
He made a wedding cake of the haystack in the
field,
He dredged the countryside and the grass was all
concealed,
He sprinkled sugar on the roofs, in patches not too
neat,
And in the morning when we woke, the world
around was sweet.

Wake up Amy

Wake up, Amy chile,
water fe get,
the barrel fe full an'
we no draw one pan yet,
an' me see de sun
a-come up over de hill,
ah know if I lef'
yuh gwine be sleepin' still
at half past ten,
maybe twelve o'clock,
if yuh don't hurry up,
de school gate gwine lock,
before yuh get dere,
we haffe look firewood,
comb we hair,
give de goat dem food,
tie out de donkey,
sweep de yard,
an' eat breakfast,
I know it hard
Fe leave you
Nice warm bed,
But work dey fe do,
Get up, sleepyhead!

Wake up, wake up, wake up beeny bud
Wake up, beeny soon o' mawnin',
Wake up, wake up, wake up beeny bud
Wake up, beeny soon o' mawnin'.

My Sister Thinks I'm Hopeless

My sister thinks I'm hopeless,
My sister thinks I'm dim,
She's given me many lessons,
But still I cannot swim.

I cannot do the backstroke,
I cannot do the crawl,
I cannot do the butterfly
Or the breaststroke, not at all.

My sister's losing patience,
She's shown me how to move,
To stretch my arms and kick my legs,
And she says she doesn't approve

Of how easily I give up,
She says I'm such a knuckle head.
But I think it's really very hard
To learn to swim in bed.

Valerie Bloom

First Contact

The thick hair caressed her back
As she lifted her head,
And stared.

She reached her hand,
Annatto-stained, to the shoulder
Of her small dumb dog.

The parrots, for once,
Were silent,
Breaking off their bickering
To stare with her

Across the blue stillness,
To the three squares of white
Skirting the horizon.

She watched them race closer,
Big-bellied with the wind,
Saw the elaborate canoes beneath.

They were like nothing she had seen before,
So she dropped her digging stick,
And ran.

Autumn Gilt

The late September sunshine
Lime green on the linden leaves
Burns bronze on the slated roof-tops,
Yellow on the farmer's last sheaves.
It flares flame-like on the fire hydrant,
Is ebony on the blackbird's wing,
Blue beryl on the face of the ocean,
Glints gold on the bride's wedding ring.
A sparkling rainbow on the stained-glass window,
It's a silver sheen on the kitchen sink,
The late September sunshine
Is a chameleon, I think.

William Wordsworth

William Wordsworth (1770–1850) is one of the Romantic poets and was friends with Samuel Taylor Coleridge, with whom he collaborated on *Lyrical Ballads*, which includes Wordsworth's poem 'Tintern Abbey'. Wordsworth was orphaned at the age of thirteen, and was sent to school in the Lake District and then to Cambridge. It is here that he developed radical political views and was a great supporter of the French Revolution. Both of these factors have a great influence on his poems, which are often about imagination, freedom and nature. His most famous poems are 'The Prelude', 'Daffodils' and 'Upon Westminster Bridge'.

Daffodils

I wander'd lonely as a cloud
  That floats on high o'er vales and hills,
When all at once I saw a crowd,
  A host of golden daffodils;
Beside the lake, beneath the trees,
Fluttering and dancing in the breeze.

Continuous as the stars that shine
  And twinkle on the Milky Way,
They stretch'd in never-ending line
  Along the margin of a bay:
Ten thousand saw I at a glance,
Tossing their heads in sprightly dance.

The waves beside them danced, but they
  Out-did the sparkling waves in glee:
A poet could not but be gay,
  In such a jocund company:
I gazed – and gazed – but little thought
What wealth the show to me had brought:

For oft, when on my couch I lie
  In vacant or in pensive mood,
They flash upon that inward eye
  Which is the bliss of solitude;
And then my heart with pleasure fills,
And dances with the daffodils.

Upon Westminster Bridge

Earth has not anything to show more fair:
Dull would he be of soul who could pass by
A sight so touching in its majesty:
This City now doth, like a garment, wear
The beauty of the morning; silent, bare,
Ships, towers, domes, theatres, and temples lie
Open unto the fields, and to the sky;
All bright and glittering in the smokeless air.
Never did sun more beautifully steep
In his first splendour, valley, rock, or hill;
Ne'er saw I, never felt, a calm so deep!
The river glideth at his own sweet will:
Dear God! the very houses seem asleep;
And all the mighty heart is lying still!

A Change in the Year

It is the first mild day of March:
  Each minute sweeter than before,
The redbreast sings from the tall larch
  That stands beside our door.

There is a blessing in the air,
  Which seems a sense of joy to yield
To the bare trees, and mountains bare;
  And grass in the green field.

The Kitten at Play

See the kitten on the wall,
Sporting with the leaves that fall,
Withered leaves, one, two and three,
Falling from the elder-tree;
Through the calm and frosty air
Of the morning bright and fair.

See the kitten, how she starts,
Crouches, stretches, paws and darts;
With a tiger-leap half way
Now she meets her coming prey.
Lets it go as fast and then
Has it in her power again.

Now she works with three and four,
Like an Indian conjuror;
Quick as he in feats of art,
Gracefully she plays her part;
Yet were gazing thousands there,
What would little Tabby care?

She Dwelt Among the Untrodden Ways

She dwelt among the untrodden ways
   Beside the springs of Dove,
A Maid whom there were none to praise
   And very few to love:

A violet by a mossy stone
   Half-hidden from the eye!
– Fair as a star, when only one
   Is shining in the sky.

She lived unknown, and few could know
   When Lucy ceased to be;
But she is in her grave, and, oh,
   The difference to me!

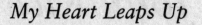

Saturday

My Heart Leaps Up

My heart leaps up when I behold
  A rainbow in the sky:
So was it when my life began;
So is it now I am a man;
So be it when I shall grow old,
  Or let me die!
The Child is father of the Man;
And I could wish my days to be
Bound each to each by natural piety.

Sunday

To the Small Celandine

Pansies, lilies, kingcups, daisies,
Let them live upon their praises;
Long as there's a sun that sets,
Primroses will have their glory;
Long as there are violets,
They will have a place in story:
There's a flower that shall be mine,
'Tis the little Celandine.

John Rice

John Rice grew up in a seaside town in Scotland. Luckily for him he was never eaten for pudding by the Loch Ness Monster ('Rice' – get it?). He started writing poems when he was very young and published his first poems when in his early twenties. As a boy he wanted to be an astronaut and would often sit at the back of the class designing and drawing rocket ships. He still reads lots of books about space and astronomy and hopes to be the First Poet on the Moon one day (or the first poet to have a drink in the Mars Bar!). John lives in the south-east of England, but spends a lot of time in Scotland, walking in the mountains, mucking about in boats or just taking photographs of the scenery. He particularly enjoys watching the seabirds – puffins, skuas, gannets, kittiwakes – who live on the sheer cliffs. He says it's fascinating to watch these great 'seabird cities': there's lots of coming and going, rushing and pushing, screeching and screaming with the young birds giving the adult birds a hard time – just like school really! John has written thirteen books and performed his poetry at hundreds of schools, libraries, festivals and book events all over Britain. He has two grown-up sons and a daughter. His favourite things include pasta, Saturdays and the Atlantic Ocean. He always washes his legs before sitting down to dinner (just in case there's someone important under the table).

Constant, Constant, Little Light

(a twenty-first-century version of Jane Taylor's poem 'The Star', now universally known as the nursery rhyme 'Twinkle, twinkle little star')

Constant, constant, little light,
catch my eye in darkest night.
What can speed so fast, so high,
laser like across the sky?

When the sleepy sun has set
and the night has cast her net,
It's then your orbit forms a ring,
round the earth a song to sing.

Constant, constant, little light,
I know you're a satellite.

Cruising, spinning, seldom seen,
beaming pictures to our screens.
Weather-watching, tracking storms,
plotting maps and all life forms.

Scanning, spying from above,
are you hawk or are you dove?
Silent, stealthy space-age Thor,
armed with weapons for a real star war.

From your tiny, silver glow,
who can tell what wrongs may flow?
But for now I hold you bright,
constant, constant, little light.

Constant, constant, little light,
I know you're a satellite.

On Some Other Planet

On some other planet
near some other star,
there's a music-loving alien
with a big estate car.

On some other planet
on some far distant world,
there's a bright sunny garden
where a cat lies curled.

On some other planet
a trillion miles away,
there are parks and beaches
where the young aliens play.

On some other planet
in another time zone,
there are intelligent beings
who feel very much alone.

On some other planet
one that we can't see,
there must be one person
who's a duplicate of me.

Driving at Night with My Dad

Open the window,
the cool summer night swooshes in.
My favourite music playing loud.

2 a.m. – summer's midnight –
neither of us can sleep
so we go for a night drive.

Stars crowd the sky
and twinkle at us in code.
Our headlights reply in light language.

A fox crosses, red and grey,
and arches under a fence:
rabbits run and a farm cat's eyes
catch our beam.
She stares at us for a second of stretched time . . .
. . . her eyes two new coins.

Through villages that are asleep,
past farms that are warm,
past houses that are dreaming,
under trees that are resting,
past birds that have no flight, no song.

I sense I am in some other country
where day, time, people no longer matter.
In this huge dark,
through the somewhere and the nowhere
of this uninhabited world,
I feel safe and secure
driving at night with my dad.

Low Owl

Cold morn: on fork of two o'clock
owl's hoot flows from hood of wood.

Owl's song rolls from blood to brood,
owl's hoot loops on to top of town roofs,
owl's song swoops on strong doors.

Owl's slow whoop – long, forlorn –
soft flood of moon song.

*This poem is a univocalic, which means that is uses only one
of the five vowels; in this case the vowel 'o'.*

A Minute to Midnight

A minute to midnight
and all is still.

For example, these are things that are still:
ornaments, coins, lamp-posts,
the cooker, Major Clark's Home for old folk
(just opposite our house, which is also still),
the newsagent's, a hut, soap, tractors,
freshly ironed trousers draped over the chair.

A minute to midnight
and all is still
except for the things that are moving.

Like, for example,
rivers, clouds, leaves, flags,
creaky windmills, lungs, birds' feathers,
digital clocks, grass, the wind,
non-sleeping animals (especially wolves),
planet Earth, the moon, satellites in space,
toenails (well they grow, don't they),
videos that are set to record
programmes in the middle of the night,
washing lines,
mobiles above babies' cots –
and babies' eyelids, they always flicker.

Climbing the World

Heading home, the faces
of the passengers opposite
are reflected dark blue
in the late-night train windows.

I doze, my daughter yawns.

The head of the sleeping man
next to me lolls about like a puppet's.
His paperback slips from his lap
and falls on to the orange peel
he discarded before falling asleep.

He wakes in time to get off at Sevenoaks.

I pick up the book, brush the peel off the jacket.
It's *The Diary of a Young Girl: Anne Frank*,
the '97 Penguin edition, due back
at Paddington Library by 13 Dec.
I start reading the foreword

. . . Anne Frank kept a diary . . .

Her father, Otto Frank, edited her diaries
after she was dead.
I see him crying at the typewriter.

My daughter is twenty-seven.
We have great times together.
She is my friend and I love her.
Even in a train's harsh light she is very beautiful.
She is climbing the world.

Anne and Otto Frank
have taught me how to tell you this.

I shall now return the sleeping man's
book to Paddington Library.

Sunday

Castle to be Built in the Woods

1. Choose a wood.

2. Make a clearing
   near a stream.

3. Dig a moat.
   Make it deep, wide.
   Fill it with water. One bridge only.

4. Lay solid foundations for your castle.
   Then build strong buttresses, stout keeps
   and tall towers with crenellations
   around the high battlements.

5. Make sure your castle has servants such as
clerks, tailors, nurses, messengers,
damsels, brewers, and a barber.
You will need to lay down stores
of food, wine, wax, spices and herbs.

6. An airy church inside the castle grounds
and a dark dungeon deep below ground
will mean that you can have
Heaven and Hell at your fingertips.
Don't forget to stock your arsenal with
swords, daggers, lances, shields, battleaxes, etc.

7. Fire arrows at anyone who tries to
attack your castle. Build murder-holes
so that you can drop missiles and stones
on the heads of your enemies.
If you catch spies, lock them in
the smallest, narrowest, smelliest room.
Act ruthlessly. Behead people, frequently.

8. Hide treasure in a very secret part of the castle.
Lock a beautiful princess in the tower.
Force your fiercest dragon to guard both of these.
Nominate a knight who will fight your battles
so that you are never injured or endangered.
Employ a story-teller to make up tall tales
and ghost stories about your castle.
Marry someone and he can be the king.

Eleanor Farjeon

Eleanor Farjeon was one of the most important children's writers of the twentieth century. She published over eighty books of poetry, short stories, novels, plays and an autobiography. In 1956 she was awarded the Carnegie and Hans Andersen Medals and in 1959 the Regina Medal from the United States.

The Eleanor Farjeon Award is presented annually, in her memory, for outstanding service to children's literature.

It Was Long Ago

I'll tell you, shall I, something I remember?
Something that still means a great deal to me.
It was long ago.

A dusty road in summer I remember,
A mountain and an old house, and a tree
That stood, you know,

Behind the house. An old woman I remember
In a red shawl with a grey cat on her knee
Humming under a tree.

She seemed the oldest thing I can remember,
But then perhaps I was not more than three.
It was long ago.

I dragged on the dusty road, and I remember
How the old woman looked over the fence at me
And seemed to know

How it felt to be three, and called out, I remember,
'Do you like bilberries and cream for tea?'
I went under the tree

And while she hummed, and the cat purred, I remember
How she filled a saucer with berries and cream for me
So long ago,

Such berries and such cream as I remember
I never had seen before, and never see
Today, you know.

And that is almost all I can remember,
The house, the mountain, the grey cat on her knee,
Her red shawl, and the tree,
And the taste of the berries, the feel of the sun I remember,
And the smell of everything that used to be
So long ago,

Till the heat on the road outside again I remember,
And how the long dusty road seemed to have for me
No end, you know.

That is the farthest thing I can remember.
It won't mean much to you. It does to me.
Then I grew up, you see.

The Night Will Never Stay

The night will never stay,
The night will still go by,
Though with a million stars
You pin it to the sky;
Though you bind it with the blowing wind
And buckle it with the moon,
The night will slip away
Like sorrow or a tune.

Argus and Ulysses

Argus was a puppy,
Frisking full of joy.
Ulysses was his master,
Who sailed away to Troy.

Argus on the sea-shore
Watched the ship's white track,
And barked a little puppy-bark
To bring his master back.

Argus was an old dog,
Too grey and tired for tears,
He lay outside the house-door
And watched for twenty years.

When twenty years were ended
Ulysses came from Troy.
Argus wagged an old dog's wag,
And then he died for joy.

Henry VIII
1509

Bluff King Hal was full of beans;
He married half a dozen queens;
For three called Kate they cried the banns,
And one called Jane, and a couple of Annes.

The first he asked to share his reign
Was Kate of Aragon, straight from Spain –
But when his love for her was spent,
He got a divorce, and out she went.

Anne Boleyn was his second wife;
He swore to cherish her all his life –
But seeing a third he wished instead,
He chopped off poor Anne Boleyn's head.

He married the next afternoon
Jane Seymour, which was rather soon –
But after one year as his bride
She crept into her bed and died.

Anne of Cleves was Number Four;
Her portrait thrilled him to the core –
But when he met her face to face
Another royal divorce took place.

Catherine Howard, Number Five,
Billed and cooed to keep alive –
But one day Henry felt depressed;
The executioner did the rest.

Sixth and last came Catherine Parr,
Sixth and last and luckiest far –
For this time it was Henry who
Hopped the twig, and a good job too.

A Morning Song

For the First Day of Spring

Morning has broken
Like the first morning,
Blackbird has spoken
 Like the first bird.
Praise for the singing!
Praise for the morning!
Praise for them, springing
 From the first Word.

Sweet the rain's new fall
Sunlit from heaven,
Like the first dewfall
 In the first hour.
Praise for the sweetness
Of the wet garden,
Sprung in completeness
 From the first shower.

Mine is the sunlight!
Mine is the morning
Born of the one light
 Eden saw play.
Praise with elation,
Praise every morning
Spring's re-creation
 Of the First Day!

Cats

Cats sleep
Anywhere,
Any table,
Any chair,
Top of piano,
Window-ledge,
In the middle,
On the edge,
Open drawer,
Empty shoe,
Anybody's
Lap will do,
Fitted in a
Cardboard box,
In the cupboard
With your frocks –
Anywhere!
They don't care!
Cats sleep
Anywhere.

Christmas Stocking

What will go into the Christmas Stocking
While the clock on the mantelpiece goes tick-tocking?
　　An orange, a penny,
　　Some sweets, not too many,
　　A trumpet, a dolly,
　　A sprig of red holly,
　　A book and a top
　　And a grocery shop,
　　Some beads in a box,
　　An ass and an ox
　　And a lamb, plain and good,
　　All whittled in wood,
　　A white sugar dove,
　　A handful of love,
　　Another of fun,
　　And it's very near done –
　　A big silver star
　　On top – there you are!
Come morning you'll wake to the clock's tick-tocking,
And that's what you'll find in the Christmas Stocking.

Roger McGough

Born in Liverpool, Roger McGough wrote his first poem at the age of seventeen. As well as teaching, then singing on *Top of the Pops*, he has been writing and performing poems for aeons. Much travelled and translated, he is now an international ambassador for poetry and was awarded an OBE for his work in 1997. In 2001 he was honoured with the Freedom of the City of Liverpool.

He has the largest collection of missing socks in London.

Everything Touches

Everything touches, life interweaves
Starlight and wood smoke, ashes and leaves
Birdsong and thunder, acid and rain
Everything touches, unbroken chain

Rainstorm and rainbow, warrior and priest
Stingray and dolphin, beauty and beast
Heartbeat and high tide, ebb tide and flow
The universe in a crystal of snow

Snowdrop and deathcap, hangman and clown
Walls that divide come tumbling down
Seen through the night, the glimmer of day
Light is but darkness worn away

Blackness and whiteness, sunset and dawn
Those gone before, those yet to be born
Past and future, distance and time
Atom to atom, water to wine

Look all around and what do you see?
Everything touches, you're touching me
Look all around and what do you see?
Everything touches, you're touching me.

Roger McGough

The Snowman

Mother, while you were at the shops
and I was snoozing in my chair
I heard a tap at the window
saw a snowman standing there

He looked so cold and miserable
I almost could have cried
so I put the kettle on
and invited him inside

I made him a cup of cocoa
to warm the cockles of his nose
then he snuggled in front of the fire
for a cosy little doze

He lay there warm and smiling
softly counting sheep
I eavesdropped for a little while
then I too fell asleep

Seems he awoke and tiptoed out
exactly when I'm not too sure
it's a wonder you didn't see him
as you came in through the door

(oh, and by the way,
the kitten's made a puddle on the floor)

Storm

They're at it again
the wind and the rain
It all started
when the wind
took the window
by the collar
and shook it
with all its might
Then the rain
butted in
What a din
they'll be at it all night
Serves them right
if they go home in the morning
and the sky won't let them in

The Man Who Steals Dreams

Santa Claus has a brother
A fact few people know
He does not have a friendly face
Or a beard as white as snow

He does not climb down chimneys
Or ride in an open sleigh
He is not kind and giving
But cruelly takes away

He is not fond of children
Or grown-ups who are kind
And emptiness the only gift
That he will leave behind

He is wraith, he is silent
He is greyness of steam
And if you're sleeping well tonight
Then hang on to your dream

He is sour, he is stooping
His cynic's cloak is black
And if he takes your dream away
You never get it back

Dreams with happy endings
With ambition and joy
Are the ones that he seeks
To capture and destroy

So, if you don't believe in Santa
Or in anything at all
The chances are his brother
Has already paid a call

Roger McGough

What I Love about School

What I love about school
is the hurly-burly of the classroom,
the sly humour of the teachers

What I hate about teachers
is their reluctance to cartwheel
down corridors

What I love about corridors
is that the longer they are
the louder the echo

What I hate about echo echo
is its refusal to answer a straight
question question

What I love about question
is the proud admission
of its own ignorance

What I hate about ignorance
is the naive assumption
that it is bliss

What I love about bliss
is its willingness
to rhyme with kiss

What I hate about kiss
    is the news of it going around
    like wildfire

What I love about wildfire
    is its dragon's breath
    and its hunger for life

What I hate about life
    is that as soon as you get the hang of it
    you run out of time

What I love about time
    is how it flies
    except when at school

What I hate about school
    is the hurly-burly of the playground,
    the sly humour of the teachers.

Joy at the Sound

Joy at the silver birch in the morning sunshine
Joy at the spring-green of its fingertips

Joy at the swirl of cold milk in the blue bowl
Joy at the blink of its bubbles

Joy at the cat revving up on the lawn
Joy at the frogs that leapfrog to freedom

Joy at the screen that fizzes to life
Joy at The Simpsons, Lisa and Bart

Joy at the dentist: 'Fine, see you next year'
Joy at the school gates: 'Closed'

Joy at the silver withholding the chocolate
Joy at the poem, two verses to go

Joy at the zing of the strings of the racquet
Joy at the bounce of the bright yellow ball

Joy at the key unlocking the door
Joy at the sound of her voice in the hall

Give and Take

I give you clean air
You give me poisonous gas.
I give you mountains
You give me quarries.

I give you pure snow
You give me acid rain.
I give you spring fountains
You give me toxic canals.

I give you a butterfly
You gave me a plastic bottle.
I give you a blackbird
You gave me a stealth bomber.

I give you abundance
You give me waste.
I give you one last chance
You give me excuse after excuse.

Alfred, Lord Tennyson

Alfred Tennyson (1809–92) was the son of a churchman from Lincolnshire, but later in life he moved to the Isle of Wight. He first published his poetry at the age of eighteen and went on to become the best-known poet in Victorian England. Some of his poetry is said to be the most musical verse ever written in English. His most famous poems are 'The Lady of Shalott', 'The Charge of the Light Brigade' and a long narrative poem called *In Memoriam*, written after the death of his close friend, Lord Alfred Douglas. Queen Victoria found it a great comfort after her husband died, and apparently kept a copy of it by her bedside.

Minnie and Winnie

Minnie and Winnie
  Slept in a shell.
Sleep, little ladies!
  And they slept well.

Pink was the shell within,
  Silver without;
Sounds of the great sea
  Wandered about.

Sleep, little ladies,
  Wake not soon!
Echo on echo
  Dies to the moon.

Two bright stars
  Peeped into the shell.
'What are they dreaming of?
  Who can tell?'

Started a green linnet
  Out of the croft;
Wake, little ladies,
  The sun is aloft!

The Lady of Shalott

PART I

On either side the river lie
Long fields of barley and of rye,
That clothe the wold and meet the sky;
And thro' the field the road runs by
  To many-tower'd Camelot;
And up and down the people go,
Gazing where the lilies blow
Round an island there below,
  The island of Shalott.

Willows whiten, aspens quiver,
Little breezes dusk and shiver
Thro' the wave that runs for ever
By the island in the river
  Flowing down to Camelot.
Four grey walls, and four grey towers,
Overlook a space of flowers,
And the silent isle imbowers
  The Lady of Shalott.

By the margin, willow-veil'd,
Slide the heavy barges trail'd
By slow horses; and unhail'd
The shallop flitteth silken-sail'd
      Skimming down to Camelot:
But who hath seen her wave her hand?
Or at the casement seen her stand?
Or is she known in all the land,
      The Lady of Shalott?

Only reapers, reaping early
In among the bearded barley,
Hear a song that echoes cheerly
From the river winding clearly,
      Down to tower'd Camelot:
And by the moon the reaper weary,
Piling sheaves in uplands airy,
Listening, whispers ''Tis the fairy
      Lady of Shalott.'

PART II
There she weaves by night and day
A magic web with colours gay.
She has heard a whisper say,
A curse is on her if she stay
      To look down to Camelot.
She knows not what the curse may be,
And so she weaveth steadily,
And little other care hath she,
      The Lady of Shalott.

And moving thro' a mirror clear
That hangs before her all the year,
Shadows of the world appear.
There she sees the highway near
       Winding down to Camelot:
There the river eddy whirls,
And there the surly village-churls,
And the red cloaks of market girls,
       Pass onward from Shalott.

Sometimes a troop of damsels glad,
An abbot on an ambling pad,
Sometimes a curly shepherd-lad,
Or long-hair'd page in crimson clad,
       Goes by to tower'd Camelot;
And sometimes thro' the mirror blue
The knights come riding two and two:
She hath no loyal knight and true,
       The Lady of Shalott.

But in her web she still delights
To weave the mirror's magic sights,
For often thro' the silent nights
A funeral, with plumes and lights,
       And music, went to Camelot:
Or when the moon was overhead,
Came two young lovers lately wed;
'I am half sick of shadows,' said
       The Lady of Shalott.

PART III
A bow-shot from her bower-eaves,
He rode between the barley-sheaves,
The sun came dazzling thro' the leaves,
And flamed upon the brazen greaves
      Of bold Sir Lancelot.
A red-cross knight for ever kneel'd
To a lady in his shield,
That sparkled on the yellow field,
      Beside remote Shalott.

The gemmy bridle glitter'd free,
Like to some branch of stars we see
Hung in the golden Galaxy.
The bridle bells rang merrily
      As he rode down to Camelot:
And from his blazon'd baldric slung
A mighty silver bugle hung,
And as he rode his armour rung,
      Beside remote Shalott.

All in the blue unclouded weather
Thick-jewell'd shone the saddle-leather,
The helmet and the helmet-feather
Burn'd like one burning flame together,
      As he rode down to Camelot.
As often thro' the purple night,
Below the starry clusters bright,
Some bearded meteor, trailing light,
      Moves over still Shalott.

His broad clear brow in sunlight glow'd;
On burnish'd hooves his war-horse trode;
From underneath his helmet flow'd
His coal-black curls as he rode,
      As he rode down to Camelot.
From the bank and from the river
He flash'd into the crystal mirror,
'Tirra lira,' by the river
      Sang Sir Lancelot.

She left the web, she left the loom,
She made three paces thro' the room,
She saw the water-lily bloom,
She saw the helmet and the plume,
      She look'd down to Camelot.
Out flew the web and floated wide;
The mirror crack'd from side to side;
'The curse is come upon me,' cried
      The Lady of Shalott.

PART IV
In the stormy east-wind straining,
The pale yellow woods were waning,
The broad stream in his banks complaining,
Heavily the low sky raining
      Over tower'd Camelot;
Down she came and found a boat
Beneath a willow left afloat,
And round about the prow she wrote
      The Lady of Shalott.

And down the river's dim expanse –
Like some bold seër in a trance,
Seeing all his own mischance –
With a glassy countenance
        Did she look to Camelot.
And at the closing of the day
She loosed the chain, and down she lay;
The broad stream bore her far away,
        The Lady of Shalott.

Lying, robed in snowy white
That loosely flew to left and right –
The leaves upon her falling light –
Thro' the noises of the night
        She floated down to Camelot:
And as the boat-head wound along
The willowy hills and fields among,
They heard her singing her last song,
        The Lady of Shalott.

Heard a carol, mournful, holy,
Chanted loudly, chanted lowly,
Till her blood was frozen slowly,
And her eyes were darken'd wholly,
        Turn'd to tower'd Camelot.
For ere she reach'd upon the tide
The first house by the water-side,
Singing in her song she died,
        The Lady of Shalott.

Under tower and balcony,
By garden-wall and gallery,
A gleaming shape she floated by,
Dead-pale between the houses high,
      Silent into Camelot.
Out upon the wharfs they came,
Knight and burgher, lord and dame,
And round the prow they read her name,
      The Lady of Shalott.

Who is this? and what is here?
And in the lighted palace near
Died the sound of royal cheer;
And they cross'd themselves for fear,
      All the knights at Camelot:
But Lancelot mused a little space;
He said, 'She has a lovely face;
God in his mercy lend her grace,
      The Lady of Shalott.'

The Eagle

He clasps the crag with crooked hands;
Close to the sun in lonely lands,
Ring'd with the azure world, he stands.

The wrinkled sea beneath him crawls;
He watches from his mountain walls,
And like a thunderbolt he falls.

The Charge of the Light Brigade

I

Half a league, half a league,
  Half a league onward,
All in the valley of Death
  Rode the six hundred.
'Forward, the Light Brigade!
Charge for the guns!' he said;
Into the valley of Death
  Rode the six hundred.

II

'Forward, the Light Brigade!'
Was there a man dismay'd?
Not tho' the soldier knew
  Some one had blunder'd:
Theirs not to make reply,
Theirs not to reason why,
Theirs but to do and die:
Into the valley of Death
  Rode the six hundred.

III

Cannon to right of them,
Cannon to left of them,
Cannon in front of them
    Volley'd and thunder'd;
Storm'd at with shot and shell,
Boldly they rode and well,
    Into the jaws of Death,
    Into the mouth of Hell
    Rode the six hundred.

IV

Flash'd all their sabres bare,
Flash'd as they turn'd in air,
Sabring the gunners there,
Charging an army, while
    All the world wonder'd:
Plunged in the battery-smoke
Right thro' the line they broke;
    Cossack and Russian
Reel'd from the sabre-stroke
    Shatter'd and sunder'd.
Then they rode back, but not,
    Not the six hundred.

V

Cannon to right of them,
Cannon to left of them,
Cannon behind them
    Volley'd and thunder'd;
Storm'd at with shot and shell,
While horse and hero fell,
They that had fought so well
Came thro' the jaws of Death
Back from the mouth of Hell,
All that was left of them,
    Left of six hundred.

VI

When can their glory fade?
O the wild charge they made!
    All the world wonder'd.
Honour the charge they made!
Honour the Light Brigade,
    Noble six hundred!

Break, break, break

Break, break, break
  On thy cold grey stones, O Sea!
And I would that my tongue could utter
  The thoughts that arise in me.

O well for the fisherman's boy,
  That he shouts with his sister at play!
O well for the sailor lad,
  That he sings in his boat on the bay!

And the stately ships go on
  To their haven under the hill;
But O for the touch of a vanish'd hand,
  And the sound of a voice that is still!

Break, break, break
  At the foot of thy crags, O Sea!
But the tender grace of a day that is dead
  Will never come back to me.

Alfred, Lord Tennyson

The Kraken

Below the thunders of the upper deep;
Far far beneath in the abysmal sea,
His ancient, dreamless, uninvaded sleep
The Kraken sleepeth: faintest sunlights flee
About his shadowy sides: above him swell
Huge sponges of millennial growth and height;
And far away into the sickly light,
From many a wondrous grot and secret cell
Unnumber'd and enormous polypi
Winnow with giant fins the slumbering green.
There hath he lain for ages and will lie
Battening upon huge seaworms in his sleep,
Until the latter fire shall heat the deep;
Then once by men and angels to be seen,
In roaring he shall rise and on the surface die.

Crossing the Bar

Sunset and evening star,
  And one clear call for me.
And may there be no moaning of the bar,
  When I put out to sea,

But such a tide as moving seems asleep,
  Too full for sound and foam,
When that which drew from out the boundless deep
  Turns again home.

Twilight and evening bell,
  And after that the dark:
And may there be no sadness of farewell,
  When I embark;

For tho' from out our bourne of Time and Place
  The flood may bear me far,
I hope to see my Pilot face to face,
  When I have crost the bar.

Andrew Fusek Peters

Andrew Fusek Peters is Britain's tallest poet – six foot eight (and a half). Since 1987 he has been performing his mad poems and playing that didgeridoo in schools, libraries and on radio and television – though he never got a badge from *Blue Peter*! With his wife, Polly, he has written and edited over thirty-five books for young people, many critically acclaimed. Check him out on www.tallpoet.com.

E-Pet-Aph

Gerbil Gerry made a mess
When he got trapped in the trouser press.
It's sad to say, the truth is that
Both of us now feel quite flat.
Poor old pet with a permanent crease,
Gerry Gerbil, *Pressed In Peace*.

Poem for the Verbally Confused

Got up, Boiled the bed,
Took a train downstairs,
Feeling live-tired and with such a baking head.

Drank not one shredded wheat but three,
Then I Grew myself a nice cup of tea,
Planted some toast, Watered the eggs,
Sat down in a chair and Ate my legs.

Crushed my teeth, Smashed my face,
Poached my hair till I Looked dead ace!
Dug my way to school,
And after Went for a Snog in the local Snogging Pool!

Caught the bus, Put it in my pocket,
My mum Made a fuss and Told me to Return it.
Killed my homework, which Was very Satisfying,
Especially when all the answers Were Writhing around and
    Dying!

In the end, I Pounded into bed,
Cut off my tired and weary head
And Swam down deep into soft and silent sleep . . .

The Gold-Leaf Gangster

Autumn:
Summer sighed,
sat down
And Winter offered her a cup of tea.

Autumn:
Summer's gone, took her summer holiday.

Autumn:
friend of sly Winter,
The Gold-Leaf Gangster.
This man is wanted for tree-stripping
And stealing Summer's colour TV.
For the next three months,
It's only black and white.

Autumn:
Summer's so sad
she went out for a night on the town
and afterwards,
couldn't remember a thing.

Hot and bothered Nature
bought an air freshener.
But cool Winter got a bit too fresh,
made his big mistake
when he kissed the sleeping beauty,
Spring!

Fire at Night

It's ready steady sticks for fiery fun,
The strike of the match is the starter's gun.
Up go the flames, long-jumping sky,
The smoke catches up, hurdling high.
The crowd stamp their frozen feet,
Clap their hands for the winning heat.
Guy Fawkes sits on top of the pyre,
Easily beaten, eaten by fire.
Who is quickest in the scorching race?
Flames of gold grab first place.
Who beat the day? The crowd then roars;
The moon made silver to the stars' applause.
Who has come third? No one remembers,
As they all sprint home, leaving only bronze embers.
As clouds shuffle by with a marathon creep,
Children in bed clutch the prize of sleep.

The Teflon Terror

I know that the monster without a head
Is lying in wait right under my bed
But being headless, he can't see
What I've brought upstairs with me.
This frying pan should do the trick.
BANG!
(Thank God that monster was non-stick!)

Andrew Fusek Peters

Rap up My Lunch

This is the lunchtime slip slop rap
Spaghetti hoops or sausage in a bap.
Click your fingers, stamp your feet
Groovy gravy, two veg, no meat.
Shake your body, swivel those hips,
Salt and vinegar, fish and chips.
Hold your hands up in the air,
Chocolate custard, apple or pear.
Feel that beat, you're on the loose,
Lemonade or orange juice.
Chatter clatter, make a noise,
No more hungry girls and boys.
Rhythm and rap to the roasting rhyme,
Lunch is done, it's playtime.

The Letter

Begun with a word
Spun from the heart
To click the pen
And make it start.

Out pours ink
To the alphabet sea,
Whales of words
Racing free.

Now my words are done
So wrap them tight
In an envelope
Of night.

Stamp a head
On to its face,
Dressed with address
Slotted in place . . .

Till along comes burglar
With sack and key
To steal the words
To you from me.

Sack to van
And van to train
Into the night,
Words like rain,

Falling through tunnels
And grumbling towns;
Sidings, hiding
Smiles and Frowns.

Slow train, night train
Cradle of words,
Rocking on tracks
Through sleepy suburbs.

Screech to a full stop
Stationery halted,
Words of the thwarted
Courted, sorted.

Van to Sack
And sack to fist,
Pushed through doors
With a twist of the wrist.

Shepherd Postman,
Delivering herds,
A flock of letters
Bleating words.

Head feels woolly
At break of day;
Here comes the post,
Now what will it say?

Rip the envelope,
Pour out my heart.
Must write back,
But where shall I start?

Gervase Phinn

Gervase Phinn leads a very full and busy life: he is a teacher, freelance lecturer, author, poet, schools inspector, broadcaster, educational consultant and professor of education. He has become one of Britain's best-loved comic writers.

Today, I Feel

Today, I feel as:

Pleased as PUNCH,
Fit as a FIDDLE,
Keen as a KNIFE,
Hot as a GRIDDLE,
Bold as BRASS,
Bouncy as a BALL,
Keen as MUSTARD,
High as a WALL,
Bright as a BUTTON,
Light as a FEATHER,
Fresh as a DAISY,
Fragrant as HEATHER,
Chirpy as a CRICKET,
Sound as a BELL,
Sharp as a NEEDLE,
Deep as a WELL,
High as a KITE,
Strong as a BULL,
Bubbly as BATH WATER,
Warm as WOOL,
Clean as a new PIN,
Shiny as MONEY,
Quick as LIGHTNING,
Sweet as HONEY,
Cool as a CUCUMBER,
Fast as a HARE,
Right as RAIN,

Brave as a BEAR,
Lively as a MONKEY,
Busy as a BEE,
Good as GOLD,
Free as the SEA.

I'M SO HAPPY – I'M JUST LOST FOR WORDS.

Visitor

The day after they mowed the meadow
Behind our house,
A mouse
Appeared.
It poked its curious black-eyed whiskered face out
From behind the gas fire
And watched us watching television.
It joined us later for tea,
Nibbling the crumbs which fell from the table
Without a by your leave
And then returned to the dark warmth behind the gas fire.
Impudent rodent!
I have not the heart to set a trap.

Gervase Phinn

Fireworks

Flames illuminate the night,
Iridescent blossoms fall to earth,
Red flowers burst into life,
Explosions of glittering teardrops rain down,
Whirling patterns dance across the sky,
Overhead, spinning shapes disperse into the darkness,
Rainbows appear high above,
Kaleidoscopes of dazzling colour,
Shimmering showers of silver.

Using Your Imagination

On Monday Miss More
Said we could paint a picture
And all use our imaginations.
I drew a dragon,
In a dark and dripping cave,
With yellow scaly skin
And slithery, snake-like tail,
Blue fins and bone-white horns,
Red-eyed and breathing purple flames.
But Miss More, when she saw it, sighed and said:
'Daniel dear, dragons are not yellow
They are green!'

With Bells On

Now, if you are all looking this way, children, I am going to tell you the story of Christmas.

I've heard it, Miss.

Yes, I know that you have heard it, Briony, we have all heard it, dear, and we are all going to hear it again.

Why, Miss?

Because we are. It's a very special story, so special, in fact, that it is well worth repeating. Now, sit up smartly, children, nice straight backs, eyes this way, and we will begin. It was a cold, cold winter night many, many years ago when Mary and Joseph arrived in Bethlehem. Joseph walked ahead, holding up his lantern to light the way.

Didn't he have a torch, Miss?

No, Kimberley, he didn't have a torch. There were no torches in those days. Mary was on an old donkey which walked oh so slowly. Clip-clop, clip-clop he went. I think he knew that he was carrying a very precious burden that night.

Miss, we live next door to Mrs Burdon.

This is a different burden, Patrick. This burden was a very heavy weight.

Mrs Burdon's very heavy, Miss. My mum says she's fat.

Patrick, dear, just listen. This story has nothing to do with Mrs Burdon. As I was saying, Mary was on an old donkey which walked oh so slowly. Clip-clop, clip-clop he went.

Miss, I went on a donkey this year at Blackpool. It ran off along the sands and my dad had to chase it. It kicked my dad and tried to bite him, Miss.

Yes, well, this donkey was a very special donkey, Dean, a very gentle donkey.

Did it have bells on, Miss?

No, it didn't have bells on.

Didn't they have bells in those days, Miss?

I'm sure they did have bells, Dean, but this donkey didn't have any.

The donkey I went on at Blackpool had bells on.

Yes, well, this one didn't, Dean. Now, Mary knew she was going to have a baby very soon. She had been travelling all day and she felt very very tired.

Miss, my dad was very very tired after he chased the donkey.

Mary was tired because she had been travelling all day and was having a baby.

Miss, my Auntie Brenda felt very tired when she was having my cousin Oliver. She had swollen ankles and a bad back and, Miss, she was always being sick. She said it was the last baby she was going to have because . . .

Patrick, just listen, dear. Mary and Joseph had been waiting so long for the arrival of their very special baby.

Nine months!

That's right, Patrick. My goodness, you do know a lot about babies.

Miss, I know where babies come from as well. My dad told me.

Yes, well, this is not the time nor the place to go into that.

Did she go to the hospital, Miss?

No, she didn't. There were no hospitals in those days.

Miss, my Auntie Brenda had to go to the hospital.

Well, Mary didn't. Now just listen, there's a good boy. My goodness, we will never get through the story with all these interruptions. Joseph looked everywhere for somewhere to stay. He asked at the inn but the innkeeper said that there was no room. There was only the stable where the ox and the ass slept.

Miss, what's an ass?

It's a donkey, Briony.

I wouldn't like to sleep with a donkey, Miss. The one in Blackpool was really smelly and tried to kick my dad and bite his hand.

Dean, this was a very nice donkey in the stable. Soon Mary would have her very special baby and lay him in swaddling clothes in a manger.

The donkeys in Blackpool were mangy, Miss. My dad said.

I said manger, Dean, not mangy. The Angel told Mary not to fear. He brought tidings of great joy, but he told Joseph to take Mary and the baby and flee to Egypt.

Miss, the donkeys in Blackpool had fleas, Miss. My Auntie Christine was scratching the whole holiday and . . .

I think we will finish the story tomorrow, children. Now, sit up smartly, nice straight backs, eyes this way, and we will wait for the bell.

Grandmother

My grandmother travelling in Spain,
Fell from a fast-moving train.
She bounced down the track,
And when she climbed back,
Exclaimed: 'Could I do that again?'

All Creatures

I just can't seem to help it,
I love creatures – great and small,
But it's ones that others do not like
I love the best of all.
I like creepy-crawly beetles
And shiny black-backed bugs,
Gnats and bats and spiders,
And slimy fat black slugs.
I like chirpy little crickets
And buzzing bumblebees,
Lice and mice and ladybirds,
And tiny jumping fleas.
I like wasps and ants and locusts,
Centipedes and snails,
Moles and voles and earwigs
And rats with long pink tails.
I like giant moths with dusty wings
And maggots fat and white,
Worms and germs and weevils,
And fireflies in the night.
No, I just can't seem to help it,
To me not one's a pest,
It's ones that others do not like,
I seem to love the best.
So it makes it rather difficult,
It's enough to make me cry,
Because my job's in pest control,
And I just couldn't hurt a fly.

Emily Dickinson

Emily Dickinson was born in Massachusetts, USA, in 1830. She had an academic education and was lively and sociable in her twenties. However, she slowly retreated into her house and refused to go out.

She wrote poems from her early childhood, but only seven were seen in her lifetime. When she died, over two thousand intense, dazzling poems were found. One of her most famous poems is 'I'm Nobody, Who Are You?'

She is famous for her use of hyphens!

She died in 1886.

The Chariot

Because I could not stop for Death,
He kindly stopped for me;
The carriage held but just ourselves
And Immortality.

We slowly drove, he knew no haste,
And I had put away
My labor, and my leisure too,
For his civility.

We passed the school where children played,
Their lessons scarcely done;
We passed the fields of grazing grain,
We passed the setting sun.

We paused before a house that seemed
A swelling of the ground;
The roof was scarcely visible,
The cornice but a mound.

Since then 't is centuries; but each
Feels shorter than the day
I first surmised the horses' heads
Were toward eternity.

To *Make a Prairie*

To make a prairie it takes a clover and one bee,
One clover, and a bee,
And revery.
The revery alone will do,
If bees are few.

The Moon

The moon was but a chin of gold
A night or two ago,
And now she turns her perfect face
Upon the world below.

It's All I Have

It's all I have to bring to-day,
This, and my heart beside,
This, and my heart, and all the fields,
And all the meadows wide.
Be sure you count, should I forget, –
Some one the sum could tell, –
This, and my heart, and all the bees
Which in the clover dwell.

Hope

Hope is the thing with feathers
That perches in the soul,
And sings the tune without the words,
And never stops at all,

And sweetest in the gale is heard;
And sore must be the storm
That could abash the little bird
That kept so many warm.

I've heard it in the chillest land,
And on the strangest sea;
Yet, never, in extremity,
It asked a crumb of me.

March

Dear March – Come In –
How glad I am –
I hoped for you before –
Put down your Hat –
You must have walked –
How out of Breath you are –
Dear March, how are you, and the Rest –
Did you leave Nature well –
Oh March, Come right up stairs with me –
I have so much to tell –

I got your Letter, and the Birds –
The Maples never knew that you were coming – till I called
I declare – how Red their Faces grew –
But March, forgive me – and
All those Hills you left for me to Hue –
There was no Purple suitable –
You took it all with you –

Who knocks? That April.
Lock the Door –
I will not be pursued –
He stayed away a Year to call
When I am occupied –
But trifles look so trivial
As soon as you have come

That Blame is just as dear as Praise
And Praise as mere as Blame –

A Slash of Blue

A slash of Blue –
A sweep of Gray –
Some scarlet patches on the way,
Compose an Evening Sky –
A little purple – slipped between
Some Ruby Trousers hurried on –
A Wave of Gold –
A Bank of Day –
This just makes out the Morning Sky.

Robert Louis Stevenson

Robert Louis Stevenson was born in 1850. While he was growing up in Edinburgh, Scotland, his parents hoped that he would become a lawyer. Luckily for us he went against his parents' wishes and, instead, became a highly successful writer of plays, novels, poetry, and children's stories like *Treasure Island* and *The Strange Case of Dr Jekyll and Mr Hyde*. However, he also wrote much poetry, which was published in *A Child's Garden of Verses* in 1885. Despite his successful career, he never enjoyed full health, and he and his family eventually left his cherished hills of Scotland and travelled to the Pacific, settling in Samoa for a healthier lifestyle. He died after only four years there, in 1894.

Skye Boat Song

Sing me a song of a lad that is gone,
　Say, could that lad be I?
Merry of soul he sailed on a day
　Over the sea to Skye.

Mull was astern, Rum on the port,
　Eigg on the starboard bow;
Glory of youth glowed in his soul:
　Where is that glory now?

Sing me a song of a lad that is gone,
　Say, could that lad be I?
Merry of soul he sailed on a day
　Over the sea to Skye.

Give me again all that was there,
　Give me the sun that shone!
Give me the eyes, give me the soul,
　Give me the lad that's gone!

Sing me a song of a lad that is gone,
　Say, could that lad be I?
Merry of soul he sailed on a day
　Over the sea to Skye.

Billow and breeze, islands and seas,
　Mountains of rain and sun,
All that was good, all that was fair,
　All that was me is gone.

Robert Louis Stevenson

From a Railway Carriage

Faster than fairies, faster than witches,
Bridges and houses, hedges and ditches;
And charging along like troops in a battle,
All through the meadows the horses and cattle:
All of the sights of the hill and the plain
Fly as thick as driving rain;
And ever again, in the wink of an eye,
Painted stations whistle by.

Here is a child who clambers and scrambles,
All by himself and gathering brambles;
Here is a tramp who stands and gazes;
And there is the green for stringing the daisies!
Here is a cart run away in the road
Lumping along with man and load;
And here is a mill, and there is a river:
Each a glimpse and gone for ever!

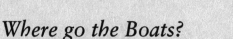
Where go the Boats?

Dark brown is the river,
  Golden is the sand.
It flows along for ever,
  With trees on either hand.

Green leaves a-floating,
  Castles of the foam,
Boats of mine a-boating –
  Where will all come home?

On goes the river,
  And out past the mill,
Away down the valley,
  Away down the hill.

Away down the river,
  A hundred miles or more,
Other little children
  Shall bring my boats ashore.

Robert Louis Stevenson

The Cow

The friendly cow, all red and white,
I love with all my heart:
She gives me cream with all her might,
To eat with apple-tart.

She wanders lowing here and there,
And yet she cannot stray,
All in the pleasant open air,
The pleasant light of day;

And blown by all the winds that pass
And wet with all the showers,
She walks among the meadow grass
And eats the meadow flowers.

The Land of Counterpane

When I was sick and lay a-bed,
I had two pillows at my head,
And all my toys beside me lay
To keep me happy all the day.

And sometimes for an hour or so
I watched my leaden soldiers go,
With different uniforms and drills,
Among the bed-clothes, through the hills;

And sometimes sent my ships in fleets
All up and down among the sheets;
Or brought my trees and houses out,
And planted cities all about.

I was the giant great and still
That sits upon the pillow-hill,
And sees before him, dale and plain,
The pleasant land of counterpane.

Robert Louis Stevenson

Happy Thought

The world is so full
  of a number of things,
I'm sure we should all
  be as happy as kings.

Bed in Summer

In winter I get up at night
And dress by yellow candle-light.
In summer, quite the other way,
I have to go to bed by day.

I have to go to bed and see
The birds still hopping on the tree,
Or hear the grown-up people's feet
Still going past me in the street.

And does it not seem hard to you,
When all the sky is clear and blue,
And I should like so much to play,
To have to go to bed by day?

Roger Stevens

Roger Stevens writes poems that are nearly always funny but are sometimes sad at the same time. Roger's favourite poem was written by his dog, Judy, a very intelligent border collie who inspired Roger's book *Taking My Human for a Walk* (Macmillan) which features poems all written by people's pets. Roger loves giving poetry performances at festivals, schools and libraries. His work appears in nearly 200 anthologies; his solo collections include *I Did Not Eat the Goldfish*, *The Monster That Ate the Universe* (both Macmillan) and *The Journal of Danny Chaucer (Poet)* (Orion) – which was broadcast on BBC Radio 4. When he's not writing, Roger plays in a blues band and runs The Poetry Zone, a website which encourages young poets at www.poetryzone.co.uk. Roger says that being a poet is the best job he's ever had, even though it's sometimes such hard work that he has to get up really early at eleven o'clock and often has to go for long walks or watch the television to get inspiration.

Sonnet Number One

The moon doth shine as bright as in the day
I sit upon the see-saw wondering why
She left me. Boys and girls come out to play.
But I'm bereft. I think I'm going to cry.
I gave her chocolate and I praised her skill
At skateboarding and football not to mention
Arm wrestling. As we slowly climbed the hill
To fetch some water, did I sense a tension?
She seemed preoccupied. She hardly spoke
And as we turned the handle to the well
I asked her, Jill, please tell me it's a joke.
She said, I've found another bloke. I fell,
I rolled, head over heels into the dark
Down to the bottom where I broke my heart

When Dad Went into Space

What was it like in space, Dad?
You've seen the snaps, he said.
Like being in a giant church
Or rising from the dead

The colours were much brighter
Louder and somehow scented
To tell you properly I'd need words
That haven't been invented

How's it feel to be back, I asked
Dad smiled and shed a tear
The gravity – well, that's a drag
But I love the atmosphere

List of Lists

I love making lists so much
I've made a list of lists

Shopping list
Things to do today list
List of best friends you can count on
List of friends whose shoulder you can cry on
Top-ten list of fast-food stops
List of gruesome punishments
List of favourite excuses
List of favourite bands on *Top of the Pops*
List of ingredients for giant pizza
List of wishes in case a magic genie appears
List of favourite words that rhyme
Sir Bobby Robson and Sir Alex Ferguson (List of knights)
Bewildered. Shell-shocked. Confused. (List of daze)
List of presents wanted at Christmas time
List of things to do tomorrow.
And number one on tomorrow's list is . . . ?
Make a new list.

Roger Stevens

I'm Sorry

As I lie here in bed
These words swim in my head
I'm sorry

Our head teacher said
That words can't be un-said
I'm sorry

I called you maggot pie
I said, I hope you die
I'm sorry

I'm sorry for today
Tomorrow I will try to say
I'm sorry

I Did Not Eat the Goldfish

I did not eat the goldfish
It really was not me
At the time of the crime
I was sitting in a tree

I did not eat the goldfish
That's no word of a lie
I loved his silvery fins
And his glassy eye

I did not eat the goldfish
I did not touch one golden scale
And I've no idea why pondweed
Is hanging from my tail

Roger Stevens

Drum Kit for Sale

Apply to Roger Stevens

Drum Kit for Sale
Guaranteed to make house shake
Very Loud Indeed
(Gave Mum a headache)

Drum Kit for sale
Snappy snare – terrific tone
Dad says – Must go at any price!

(or will exchange
for trombone)

Hallowe'en

Darren's got a pumpkin
Hollowed out a treat
He put it in the window
It scared half the street

I wish I had a pumpkin
But I've not and it's a shame
I've got a scary carrot
But it's not the same

Lindsay MacRae

Lindsay MacRae is an award-winning poet. Her last three collections have been published by Puffin and her work appears in numerous anthologies. Lindsay performs her poetry throughout the country and on radio and TV. She has run workshops in schools, prisons and libraries and was Writer in Residence at the Public Record Office. She lives in London with her husband, two children and a very peculiar cat.

The Boy Who Dropped Litter

'ANTHONY WRIGGLY
SHAME ON YOU!'
screeched the teacher
as she spotted him
scrunching up his crisp packet
and dropping it carefully
on to the pavement outside school.

'If everyone went around
dropping crisp packets like you do
where would we be?'

(Anthony didn't know, so she told him)

'We'd be wading waist-high in crisp packets,
that's where!'

Anthony was silent.
He hung his head.

It looked to the teacher
as if he was very sorry.

When in fact he was trying to calculate
just how many packets it would take
to bring Basildon to a complete standstill.

Lindsay MacRae

The Thingy

Shin kicker
Snot flicker
Crisp muncher
Shoulder huncher
Grudge bearer
Out starer
Back stabber
Biscuit grabber
Sock smeller
Fib teller
Thinks that it's
Uri Geller.

Loud belcher
Slug squelcher
Pillow drooler
I'm the ruler
Gonna beat yer
That'll teach yer
Bog ugly
Swamp creature
Found mainly
Under-cover
What is it?

MY BROTHER!

2 Poems about 4 Eyes

They call me Specky Four Eyes.
I wear glasses, so it's true,
I can see quite well why you're teasing me,
I've got two more eyes than you.

My spectacles are magical
for when you taunt and jeer,
I only have to take them off
to make you disappear.

Lindsay MacRae

The Fruit Sticker Sorcerer

More of a magician
than a second dad.
When my friends ask me what he does
I say that he conjures magic from the weekly shop.
That it's like gliding with Merlin
down a supermarket aisle.
I watch him delighted from my Tesco chariot,
peeling foreign countries
from the skins of fruit.
He sticks them gently
in the tiny valleys between his knuckles
and rolls down his sleeves.
Then in the dark street afterwards,
he pulls them up again.
His arms are more crowded
than a conquering general's map.
We've taken Jamaica, Israel, Guadeloupe,
several small islands in the balmy South.
Spellbound, I watch him fill the collection book
with our hoard of treasure no one else would want.
All the exotic lands I can't pronounce
shimmer in sunlight
cast by the table lamp.

Refugee

He can't speak a word of English
But the picture he paints needs no words

In it he puts:
guns
bright orange explosions
a house with no roof
children with no shoes
and his mother and father
lying still, as though asleep.
At the bottom he puts himself, tiny and dark,
with a puddle of blue tears at his feet.
Somehow the fat yellow sun at the top of the page
has a smile on its face.

Lindsay MacRae

The Long Goodbye

I'm off then
I'm leaving
Excuse me
I've just said
I'M LEAVING!
I'm bored
Of being ignored
I'M GOING
No sure where exactly
Just anywhere but here.
Look I'm serious you know
I'm actually going to go
Got my bag packed and everything
Got my toothbrush
Got a torch in case of emergencies
Got a load of cash
(in ten-pence pieces).
Bye then
Cheerio
I've gotta go
I'm going NOW
I really, really mean it
I'm actually going
I've got my coat on
I'M GOING
I'm opening the door
Don't try and stop me
I'm going

I said
I'm **REALLY** going now
I'm **REALLY**
　　　　ACTUALLY
　　　　　　　　FINALLY . . .
Right, that's it!
I'm **OFF!**
I'm slamming the door behind me
I'm slamming it again
(in case you didn't notice the first time)
What the heck
One more time for luck
I've . . .
GONE
I'm out the door
　　　　　　　through the gate
　　　　　　　　　　　　up the street
　　　　　　　　　　　　　　　round the corner
I'm in the big wide world.
You wouldn't believe
how heavy £15 in ten-pence pieces are
But I'm strong.
Right then
I'm on my way
On the road
On my own

It's raining

Perhaps I'll just phone
To tell them I'm OK
Perhaps I'll just nip back
To see how they're coping
Only joking.
It's raining
It's **REALLY, REALLY, RAINING**
I'm **REALLY COLD**
I'm **SOAKING!**
That does it!
I'm going home!
Next time I'll do it properly,
Pick a nice sunny day
in twelve years' time.
I'm back!
I said, **I'M BACK!**

Did anyone miss me?

From a Distance

I climbed to the top of the world today
and the world looked really small.
Guns and bombs and orphans' tears
couldn't be heard at all
It all looked bright and beautiful
like a cheerful Christian hymn,
with enough green fields and shady woods
to put all the people in.

I couldn't see any fences
or signs which read 'Keep Out',
nor churned up earth where tanks rolled through
to the enemy's victory shout.
And I couldn't see the eyes of a child
who has no tears left to cry,
or numb refugees at the side of the road
watch the flames from their homes light the sky.

I couldn't see the generals' smiles
as they met to divide up the land,
or hear the lies they told afterwards
with blood still warm on their hands.
I couldn't feel the sigh which leaks
from a million broken hearts
or the thick and sickening silence
before the next war starts.

I climbed to the top of the world today
and dreamed how the future could be:
the rivers unsullied by hatred and greed
and peace stretching clear to the sea.

Jan Dean

Jan Dean was brought up in Stalybridge, near Manchester, in a corner shop. Her family lived near a main road, so she wasn't allowed a bike – and her dad gave her roller skates in instalments so that she'd learn to balance on one and fall over less when she had both. Interesting theory, but it didn't work! Her mum says Jan always wanted to be a writer, but Jan doesn't remember ever saying that and thinks her mum's making it up to fit the facts.

Jan is married with two teenage sons and is the shortest person in the house, except for the dog – but she feels tall. She writes almost every day – though sometimes when she reads what she's written she can't press the delete button fast enough. Jan thinks writing is a sort of acting. When she writes she pretends all over the paper. On school visits Jan sometimes does a workshop called Acting on to Paper, and then they all pretend together!

Apart from writing and reading, Jan likes cooking – especially chocolate puddings – and singing in the church choir, though sometimes she's terrible. She's learning to paint because it makes a change from doing word stuff. Her painting is like her singing – a bit hit and miss. She can't think why she's not better at singing and painting – after all, loud and messy are two of her best things.

It's Not What I'm Used to

I don't want to go to Juniors . . .

The chairs are too big
I like my chair small, so I fit
Exactly
And my knees go
Just so
Under the table.

And that's another thing –
The tables are too big.
I like my table to be
Right
For me
So my workbook opens
Properly.
And my pencil lies in the space at the top
The way my thin cat stretches into a long line
On the hearth at home.

Pencils – there's another thing.
Another problem.
Up in Juniors they use pens and ink.
I shall really have to think

About ink.

Sheep Look White Until It Snows

In summer they are clouds on legs
White as mist
And light as candyfloss
Dotting the high hill like cotton.
But now, in January sleet
They're grey and grizzled
Under winter's drizzled slushy rain.
After frost they're dreary, stained.
Against the flurries and the drifts
They're yellower than ancient paper;
The colour of a bonfire's clotted smoke.
But every summer they still fool me
Every summer when the sun is bright
I really do believe that sheep are white.

Jan Dean

Banned

Mud's good.
But it's banned.
Because we tread in it, and then we tread it in.

The field's good.
But it's banned.
We're not allowed out on the field unless it's dry,
Which it never is.

Snow's good.
But it's banned.
Because it melts and goes to slush
And then the dirt and slush gets mushed
And makes mud.

Mud's good.
But it's banned.

Crocodile

Leathery and scaly with gold eye slits,
This old green monster grins and sits
In the steamy swamp, in the hot muddy pits –
One step nearer and I'll tear you into bits.

Got teeth. Got teeth. Got a man-trap smile
Get away. Get away. Run a long-leg mile.

The dinosaurs they came and went
They couldn't stand the pace,
But I was here before them
And I'm still around the place.
Better run – and make it snappy
Before Snappy makes it you
This is one wild crocodile who really likes to chew

Got teeth. Got teeth. Got a man-trap smile
Get away. Get away. Run a long-leg smile.

I got teeth. I got teeth. Make a shark look shy
Get away. Get away. Be a bird – just fly.
Got teeth in my heart
Got teeth in my soul
Drag you down in the water
For a dead-man roll.

Got teeth. Got teeth. Got a man-trap smile
Older than the dinosaurs – *m . . . e . . . a . . . n*
CROCODILE!

Angels

We are made from light.
Called into being we burn
Brighter than the silver white
of hot magnesium.
More sudden than yellow phosphorus.
We are the fire of heaven;
Blue flames and golden ether.

We are from stars.
Spinning beyond the farthest galaxy
In an instant gathered to this point
We shine, speak our messages and go,
Back to brilliance.
We are not separate, not individual,
We are what we are made of. Only
Shaped sometimes into tall-winged warriors,
Our faces solemn as swords,
Our voices joy.

The skies are cold;
Suns do not warm us;
Fire does not burn itself.
Only once we touched you
And felt a human heat.
Once, in the brightness of the frost.
Above the hills, in glittering starlight,
Once, we sang.

A Mother's Confession

(Or: What you have always suspected . . .)

As soon as you are asleep in bed
I unlock the secret cupboard
Where I keep all the chocolate
And I eat it and eat it and eat it.
I don't share it with anybody
And I don't give half a hoot about my teeth.

As soon as you are tucked all tidy in your bed
I put my feet up on the sofa – shoes still on,
Or if I take them off I don't undo the laces first,
Then I drink fizzy cans and eat crisps,
And practise blowing huge, round, pink bubbles
Out of hubba-bubba gum.

Once you're asleep
I watch *those* programmes on the telly
(The ones I always say are trash)
And I don't go to bed at a sensible time –
Even though I'm really, really tired.
I don't go because I'm a grown-up
And I can do what I like
And you can't stop me.
Ha. Ha. Ha.

Jan Dean

Colouring in

And staying inside the lines
Is fine, but . . .
I like it when stuff leaks –
When the blue bird and the blue sky
Are just one blur of blue blue flying,
And the feeling of the feathers in the air
And the wind along the blade of wing
Is a long gash of smudgy colour.
I like it when the flowers and the sunshine
Puddle red and yellow into orange,
The way the hot sun on my back
Lulls me – muddles me – sleepy
In the scented garden,
Makes me part of the picture . . .
Part of the place.

Pie Corbett

Pie Corbett was a primary teacher and head teacher. He once worked in the same school as the poet Brian Moses, where they ran writing clubs, published anthologies of children's poetry and pretended to teach maths while they were really writing poetry.

Pie has written and edited over a hundred books. A poet and story-teller, he spends much of his time daydreaming poems and stories. He lives in the countryside with his family, who occasionally make guest appearances in his poems. He really wanted to be a vet and work in Africa, pulling thorns out of a lion's paw! He also fancied being a spy. As a child, he kept a careful eye on the neighbours, in case they acted suspiciously. He kept well disguised with a plastic moustache and glasses!

Secret Poem

My secret is made of –
the fingertips of clouds,
the silence between heartbeats
found at a hospital bedside,
the hangman's gloves,
the stoat's bright eye,
the bullet as it slices
through the winter wind.

I found it –
on the edge of a lemon's bite,
clutched in the centre of a crocus,
held in a crisp packet,
crumpled at the side of the road
where the nettles stab
their sharp barbs
at the innocent child's hand.

This secret can –
prise open steel hearts,
smooth a stormy sea flat,
capture the wind,
cup the moon's shine
in an empty palm,
break apart Mount Everest
till it is powder
in a lover's pocket.

If I lost
this secret –
even the lonely mountain goat
would bleat . . .

The Playground Monster

It grabbed me
with its tarmac jaws
and then it tried
to bite me.

It grasped me
with its gravelly paws
and then it tried
to fight me.

I live in fear of walking
across its great black back.

I think it knows I'm talking.
It listens at a crack!

I fear its greedy darkness,
the way it seems to need

to reach out when I'm running
and grab me for a feed.

It grabbed me
with its tarmac jaws
and then it tried
to bite me.

It grasped me
with its gravelly paws
and then it tried
to fight me.

School Photo

Each summer
We were led out
on to the playing field
for the annual school photo.
The teachers sat
in a tidy row;
Miss Grainger,
grim-faced
as a baboon's backside.
The Head teacher
staring straight
into the lens,
his back like a plank.

The rest of us stood
in long rows,
the girls fussing
with their hair,
busy straightening creases,
putting on a smile.
But I was renowned for not smiling –
my mother repeatedly told me
that I had 'a face like a horse' –
so when it came to photos
I wore the mask of death.
You couldn't get
a gloomier look
this side of Scunthorpe.

That year
I was placed right on the end
of the line –
the idea was that we all stood still
while the camera panned round.
I waited till it had taken our side,
jumped down
and raced round behind
the rest of the school –
to reappear on the other end.

So there you are –
the photo shows
that year
there were identical Corbett twins –
another one of me –
standing either end of the school –
both of us
solemnly staring
into the camera,
like sad old horses.

Snakes and Fairies

There are snakes
at the bottom of our garden –
not fairies.

I found them,
coiled beneath
some corrugated iron,
basking in the heat –

As soon as
we lifted the tin
they slipped quick,
slick as a card trick,
into the grass
by our feet –

You should have seen
us scarper
to the safety
of the patio.

When I was little
I would peer
into the ears of flowers
and search beneath leaves
for the fairies
that were supposed to live
at the bottom
of our garden.

I think that the snakes
must have chased them away.

Pie Corbett

Five Ways of Looking at a Lemon

1.
It sits in the bowl
lonely as a yellow
planet.

2.
On the tongue
it is sudden and sharp
as a lie –
you shudder.

3.
A still, rancid heart,
grown cold,
plucked from the chest
of a restless man.

4.
OK, so the lemon
winked at me!

5.
The luminous lemon
lies lazily
in a languid lagoon
of light.

The Entertainment of Small Things

How entertaining –
When, stuck for the next
line in a poem,
I twang my ruler and listen
to its energy hum.

How entertaining –
When, after two hours
of listening to recipes,
my aunt puts on her hat
and leaves us alone.

How entertaining –
When, feeling lonely,
I am joined by a fly
that carefully washes
its spindly legs.

How entertaining –
When you sit
in assembly, tugging
the Velcro on your trainers
back and forth,
making a sound
like skin tearing.

Dinner time

The boys lay claim
to the playground,
staking out their territory
with sweaters.
They whoop and yell,
punching the air
as if they were stars
on *Match of the Day*.

The girls huddle to one side,
clapping rhythms,
skipping rhymes,
hop-scotching their time.

Dinner ladies,
like Sumo wrestlers,
stand guard.

The Infants steer clear
and wonder when
their mums will come
to take them home.

A lone teacher hugs
her coffee mug,
shrugs off the wind,
and casts a watchful eye.

Other kids gather in corners
to swap bubble gum cards
and jokes
they don't
understand.

Wes Magee

Wes Magee was born in Greenock, Scotland. He is a former National Serviceman, primary school teacher, and head teacher. He became a full-time author in 1989. He has published four collections of poetry for adults, and more than eighty books for young readers – fiction, poetry, plays and picture books. Wes regularly visits schools and libraries, where he leads writing workshops and performs his 'Poetry Show'. He lives in an old cottage on the North York Moors with four cats (Rusty, Eb, Flo and Kitten) and a huge pond with a population of frogs, newts and goldfish.

At the End of a School Day

It is the end of a school day
   and down the long driveway
come bag-swinging, shouting children.
   Deafened, the sky winces.
      The sun gapes in surprise.

Suddenly, the runners skid to a stop,
   stand still and stare
at a small hedgehog
   curled up on the tarmac
      like an old, frayed cricket ball.

A girl dumps her bag, tiptoes forward
   and gingerly, so gingerly
carries the creature
   to the safety of a shady hedge.
      Then steps back, watching.

Girl, children, sky and sun
   hold their breath.
There is a silence,
   a moment to remember
      on this warm afternoon in June.

I Like Emma

I like Emma
but I don't know
if she likes me.
All the boys
think I'm a fool.

I wait outside the school gate
at half past three
trying to keep my cool.
Emma walks past,
shaking her blonde hair free,
laughs with her friends
and drifts off home for tea.

Emma's two years
older than me.
Her class is higher
up the school.

I like Emma
but I don't know
if she likes me.
All the boys
think I'm a fool.

The Boneyard Rap

This is the rhythm
of the boneyard rap,
knuckle bones click
and hand bones clap,
finger bones flick
and thigh bones slap
when you're doing the rhythm
of the boneyard rap.
   Woooooooooooo!

   It's the boneyard rap
   and it's a scare.
   Give your bones a shake-up
   if you dare.
   Rattle your teeth
   and waggle your jaw
   and let's do the boneyard rap
   once more . . .

This is the rhythm
of the boneyard rap,
elbow bones clink
and backbones snap,
shoulder bones chink
and toe bones tap
when you're doing the rhythm
of the boneyard rap.
   Woooooooooooo!

It's the boneyard rap
and it's a scare.
Give your bones a shake-up
if you dare.
Rattle your teeth
and waggle your jaw
and let's do the boneyard rap
once more . . .

This is the rhythm
of the boneyard rap,
ankle bones sock
and arm bones flap,
pelvic bones knock
and knee bones zap
when you're doing the rhythm
of the boneyard rap.
Woooooooooooo!

The Day After

I went to school
the day after Dad died.
Teacher knew all about it.
She put a hand on my shoulder
    and sighed.

In class things seemed much the same
although I was strangely subdued.
Breaktime was the same too,
and at lunchtime the usual crew
played up the dinner supervisors.
Fraggle was downright rude.
I joined in the football game

but volunteered to go in goal.
That meant I was left almost alone,
could think things over on my own.
For once I let the others shout
    and race and roll.

*   *   *   *   *

First thing that afternoon,
everyone in his and her place
for silent reading,
I suddenly felt hot tears streaming
    down my face.

Salty tears splashed down
and soaked into my book's page.
Sobs heaved in my chest.
Teacher peered over her half specs
and said quietly, 'Ben, come here.'
I stood at her desk crying. At my age!
I felt like an idiot, a clown.

'Don't feel ashamed,' teacher said.
'It's only right to weep.
Here, have these tissues to keep.'
I dabbed my eyes, then looked around.
    Bowed into books, every head.

    *   *   *   *   *

'Have a cold drink.
Go with James. He'll understand.'
In the boys' cloaks I drank deeply
then slowly wiped my mouth
    on the back of my hand.

Sheepishly I said, 'My dad died.'
'I know,' said James.
'We'd best get back to class. Come on.'
Walking down the corridor I thought of Dad . . . gone.
In class no one sniggered,
they were busy getting changed for games.
No one noticed I'd cried.

All day I felt sad, sad.
After school I reached my street,
clutching the tissues, dragging my feet.
Mum was there in our house
    but no Dad,

    no Dad.

Friday

What is . . . the Sun?

The Sun is an orange dinghy
    sailing across a calm sea.

It is a gold coin
    dropped down the drain in Heaven.

The Sun is a yellow beach ball
    kicked high into the summer sky.

It is a thumbprint
    on a sheet of pale blue paper.

The Sun is a milk bottle's gold top
    floating in a puddle.

Wes Magee

The Cat with No Name

In the dingy staffroom of a school in the city,
where the teachers' damp macs hang limply from hooks,
where cracked cups are tea-stained, the worn carpet gritty,
and where there are piles of exercise books,
you will notice – at break – that the teachers don't utter
a sound. None of them grumble and none of them chat.
Why? They dare not disturb what sleeps, fat as butter,
on the staffroom's best chair: one huge tortoiseshell cat.

> For the teachers
> know very well not to wake him.
> They know that he's three parts not tame.
> He's a wild cat,
> a *wild* cat,
> a not-to-be-riled cat.
> He's the tortoiseshell cat with no name.

It was drizzly December when the cat first appeared
and took the French teacher's chair for his bed.
Now his scimitar claws in the staffroom are feared,
oh yes, *and* the street-fighter's teeth in his head.
Once a day he is seen doing arches and stretches,
then for hours like a furry coiled fossil will lie.
It's true that he's made all the staff nervous wretches.
They approach . . . and he opens one basilisk eye.

For the teachers
know very well not to stroke him.
They know that he'll not play the game.
He's a wild cat,
a *wild* cat,
a not-to-be-riled cat.
He's the tortoiseshell cat with no name.

The Headmistress, the teachers, and all the school's cleaners,
can't shift him with even a long-handled broom,
for the cat merely yawns, treats them all like has-beeners
and continues to live in that dingy staffroom.
When the French teacher tried to reclaim her armchair
with a cat-cally, shriek-squally, 'Allez-vous en!',
the cat gave a hiss, clawed the lady's long hair,
and back to Marseilles Madame Toff-Pouff has gone.

For the teachers
know very well not to irk him.
They know that he's always the same.
He's a wild cat,
a *wild* cat,
a not-to-be-riled cat.
He's the tortoiseshell cat with no name.

I once worked in that school and observed the huge
  creature's
habits as I sipped my cracked cup of weak tea.
I saw how he frightened and flummoxed the teachers,
and how – every Friday – he'd one-green-eye me.
To appease him, each day we laid out a fish dinner
which the beast snaffled up in just one minute flat
then returned to his chair with a smirk – that bad sinner!
It seems there's no way to be rid of that cat.

For the teachers
know very well not to cross him.
They know that he's three parts not tame.
He's a wild cat,
a *wild* cat,
a not-to-be-riled cat.
(He can't *bear* to be smiled at.)
He's the tortoiseshell cat with no name,
with no name.
He's the tortoiseshell cat with no name.

At the End of World War Two

To celebrate the end of the war
all the lads and lasses
have gathered at the thistly meadow
for a twenty-five-a-side football match.

The unmarked pitch slopes down
to a duckweed-covered pond
where muddied cattle drink.
White goats crop the hawthorn.

Goalposts are heaped jackets,
waistcoats and flat caps.
The ball's a pig's bladder,
inflated, and tied with twine.

Endless, the game thunders on,
on into the gloaming.
The score is nineteen-all
as the purple dusk deepens.

There are only two spectators
in the bomber-free sky:
an invalid-faced full Moon
and a single astonished star.

Richard Edwards

Richard Edwards was born and grew up in Kent. When he was young he wanted to be the Lone Ranger, Robin Hood, Rob Roy and other film and TV heroes. When he was growing up he decided to be a gardener, a teacher, a writer – specializing in poems – a detective, and a builder of odd houses. He achieved some of his ambitions, if only in his imagination.

He likes watching wild animals, reading detective stories, and eating Werther's Originals.

He started writing stories when he was eight. He hopes to go on writing until he is eighty-eight (or beyond).

The Word Party

Loving words clutch crimson roses,
Rude words sniff and pick their noses,
Sly words come dressed up as foxes,
Short words stand on cardboard boxes,
Common words tell jokes and gabble,
Complicated words play Scrabble,
Swear words stamp around and shout,
Hard words stare each other out,
Foreign words look lost and shrug,
Careless words trip on the rug,
Long words slouch with stooping shoulders,
Code words carry secret folders,
Silly words flick rubber bands,
Hyphenated words hold hands,
Strong words show off, bending metal,
Sweet words call each other 'petal',
Small words yawn and suck their thumbs
Till at last the morning comes.
Kind words give out farewell posies . . .

Snap! The dictionary closes.

Mammoths

There were mammoths in our garden last night.
What else explains
The clothesline snapped by something very strong,
The puddles shaped
Like huge feet stamped into the lawn, and all
That white blossom
Shaken from the pear tree? What else explains
The trampled rose
And the noise I heard under my window –
Huff-puffing like
A steam train going uphill in the dark?
Oh yes, there were
Mammoths in our garden last night, though these
Small signs would not
Be recognized by everyone. Only
Specialists know
What to look for, only mammoth experts,
People like me.

Bramble Talk

A caterpillar on a leaf
Said sadly to another:
'So many pretty butterflies . . .
I wonder which one's Mother.'

Richard Edwards

Ten Tall Oak Trees

Ten tall oak trees
Standing in a line,
'Warships,' cried King Henry,
Then there were nine.

Nine tall oak trees
Growing strong and straight,
'Charcoal,' breathed the furnace,
Then there were eight.

Eight tall oak trees
Reaching towards heaven,
'Sizzle,' spoke the lightning,
Then there were seven.

Seven tall oak trees,
Branches, leaves and sticks,
'Firewood,' smiled the merchant,
Then there were six.

Six tall oak trees
Glad to be alive,
'Barrels,' boomed the brewery,
Then there were five.

Five tall oak trees,
Suddenly a roar,
'Gangway!' screamed the west wind,
Then there were four.

Four tall oak trees
Sighing like the sea,
'Floorboards,' beamed the builder,
Then there were three.

Three tall oak trees
Groaning as trees do,
'Unsafe,' claimed the council,
Then there were two.

Two tall oak trees
Spreading in the sun,
'Progress,' snarled the bypass,
Then there was one.

One tall oak tree
Wishing it could run,
'Nuisance,' grumped the farmer,
Then there were none.

No tall oak trees,
Search the fields in vain,
Only empty skylines
And the cold grey rain.

Richard Edwards

Percy Pot-Shot

Percy Pot-Shot went out hunting,
Percy Pot-Shot and his gun,
Percy Pot-Shot, such a hot shot,
Shot a sparrow, said 'What fun!'

Percy Pot-Shot shot a blackbird,
Shot a lapwing, shot a duck,
Shot a swan as it rose flapping,
Shot an eagle, said 'What luck!'

Percy Pot-Shot shot a rabbit,
Shot a leaping gold-eyed hare,
Shot a tiger that lay sleeping,
Shot a rhino, shot a bear.

Percy Pot-Shot, trigger happy,
Shot a fountain, shot a tree,
Shot a river, shot a mountain,
Shot some rainclouds, shot the sea.

Percy Pot-Shot went on hunting,
Percy Pot-Shot and his gun,
Not a lot that he had not shot,
Shot the moon down, shot the sun.

Percy Pot-Shot stood in darkness,
No bird fluttered, no beast stirred,
Percy Pot-Shot knelt and muttered
'God forgive me.' No one heard.

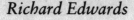

Richard Edwards

Three of a Kind

I stalk the timberland,
I wreck and splinter through,
I smash log cabins,
I wrestle grizzly bears.
At lunchtime if I'm dry
I drain a lake or two,
I send the wolves and wolverines
Howling to their lairs.
I'm Sasquatch,
Bigfoot,
Call me what you like,
But if you're a backpacker
On a forest hike,
Keep a watch behind you,
I'm there, though rarely seen.
I'm Bigfoot,
Sasquatch,
I'm mean, mean, mean.

I pad across the snow field,
Silent as a thief,
The phantom of the blizzard,
Vanishy, rare.
I haunt the barren glacier,
And men in disbelief
Goggle at the footprints
I scatter here and there.
I'm Abominable,

Yeti,
Call me what you choose,
But if you're a mountaineer,
Careful when you snooze,
I'm the restless roaming spirit
Of the Himalayan Range.
I'm Yeti,
Abominable,
I'm strange, strange, strange.

I rear up from the waves,
I thresh, I wallow,
My seven snaky humps
Leave an eerie wake.
I crunch the silly salmon,
Twenty at one swallow,
I tease the silly snoopers –
A fiend? A fish? A fake?
I'm The Monster,
Nessie,
Call me what you please,
But if you're a camper
In the lochside trees,
Before you zip your tent at night
Say your prayers and kneel.
I'm Nessie,
The Monster,
I'm real, real, real.

The Crab that Writes

When the tide is low on moonlit nights,
Out of the sea crawls the crab that writes,
Out of the sea crawls the crab whose claw
Writes these words on the shining shore:

> *Pebble mussel*
> *Fin and scale*
> *Sole and mackerel*
> *Skate and whale*
> *Seaweed starfish*
> *Salt and stone*
> *Sand and shell and cuttlebone.*

When the tide is low on moonlit nights,
Back to the sea crawls the crab that writes,
Back to the sea crawls the crab whose claw
Leaves these words on the shining shore:

> *Pebble mussel*
> *Fin and scale*
> *Sole and mackerel*
> *Skate and whale*
> *Seaweed starfish*
> *Salt and stone*
> *Sand and shell and cuttlebone.*

John Agard

John Agard was born on 21 June 1949 in Guyana. He moved to England in 1977 with his partner, the poet Grace Nichols. He worked for the Commonwealth Institute, travelling to schools throughout the UK to promote a better understanding of Caribbean culture.

In 1993 he was appointed Writer in Residence at the South Bank Centre, London, and became Poet in Residence at the BBC, an appointment created as part of a scheme run by the Poetry Society. He won the Paul Hamlyn Award for Poetry in 1997.

John has written many children's poems and books. His collection *We Animals Would Like a Word With You* received the Smarties Award. His latest collections are *Einstein, the Girl Who Hated Maths*, inspired by maths, and *Hello H$_2$O*, inspired by science. Both illustrated by Satoshi Kitamora.

John Agard

Blowing Bubbles

To you
I'm blowing bubbles.
To me
I'm conducting
an orchestra
of swirling light waves
and rainbow octaves.

To you
I'm blowing bubbles.
To me
I'm building
a nest
of planets
on a branch of breath.

Swimming Teeth

I'm not a do-as-you're-told fish.
A looked-at-in-a-bowl fish.
A stay-still-to-behold fish.
An as-you-can-guess goldfish.

Where sea is blue, I make it red.
Where body bubbles, I slash, I shred.
Where eyes see light, I blur them dark.
Where skin shines bright, I expose a heart.

Humans call me shark.
But to my friends of the deep
I am known as SWIMMING TEETH.
And one day I'd like to direct a movie.

Secret

Tell me your secret.
I promise not to tell.
I'll guard it safely at the bottom of a well.

Tell me your secret
Tell me, tell me, please.
I won't breathe a word, not even to the bees.

Tell me your secret.
It will be a pebble in my mouth.
Not even the sea can make me spit it out.

Poetry Jump-up

Tell me if Ah seeing right
Take a look down de street

Words dancin
words dancin
till dey sweat
words like fishes
jumpin out a net
words wild and free
joinin de poetry revelry
words back to back
words belly to belly

Come on everybody
come and join de poetry band
dis is poetry carnival
dis is poetry bacchanal
when inspiration call
take yu pen in yu hand
if yu don't have a pen
take yu pencil in yu hand
if yu don't have a pencil
what the hell
so long de feeling start to swell
just shout de poem out

Words jumpin off de page
tell me if Ah seein right
words like birds
jumpin out a cage
take a look down de street
words shakin dey waist
words shakin dey bum
words wit black skin
words wit white skin
words wit brown skin
words wit no skin at all
words huggin up words
an sayin I want to be a poem today
rhyme or no rhyme
I is a poem today
I mean to have a good time

Words feeling hot hot hot
big words feeling hot hot hot
lil words feeling hot hot hot
even sad words can't help
tappin dey toe
to de riddum of de poetry band

Dis is poetry carnival
dis is poetry bacchanal
so come on everybody
join de celebration
all yu need is plenty perspiration
an a little inspiration
plenty perspiration
an a little inspiration

John Agard

First Morning

I was there on that first morning of creation
when heaven and earth occupied one space
and no one had heard of the human race.

I was there on that first morning of creation
when a river rushed from the belly of an egg
and a mountain rose from a golden yolk.

I was there on that first morning of creation
when the waters parted like magic cloth
and the birds shook feathers at the first joke.

The Hurt Boy and the Birds

The hurt boy talked to the birds
and fed them the crumbs of his heart.

It was not easy to find the words
for secrets he hid under his skin.
The hurt boy spoke of a bully's fist
that made his face a bruised moon –
his spectacles stamped to ruin.

It was not easy to find the words
for things that nightly hissed
as if his pillow was a hideaway for creepy-crawlies –
the note sent to the girl he fancied
held high in mockery.

But the hurt boy talked to the birds
and their feathers gave him welcome –

Their wings taught him new ways to become.

John Agard

Don't Call Alligator Long-mouth till You Cross River

Call alligator long-mouth
call alligator saw-mouth
call alligator pushy-mouth
call alligator scissors-mouth
call alligator raggedy-mouth
call alligator bumpy-bum
call alligator all dem rude word
but better wait
             till you cross river.

Edward Thomas

Edward Thomas was born in 1878 and grew up in London. During his short adult life he attended university and was an admirer and friend of Robert Frost. He made a living from writing, but not from his poems – these were only acknowledged after his death. He only wrote poetry in the last few years of his life, and before this specialized in prose such as biographies, essays, critical studies and one novel. His poems, such as *The Heart of England* and *The South Country*, attempt to capture the essence of the English countryside which he loved so much. Unfortunately, like many of his contemporaries, his career was cut short by the First World War – he died in 1917 at the Battle of Arras.

Adlestrop

Yes. I remember Adlestrop –
The name, because one afternoon
Of heat the express-train drew up there
Unwontedly. It was late June.

The steam hissed. Someone cleared his throat.
No one left and no one came
On the bare platform. What I saw
Was Adlestrop – only the name

And willows, willow-herb, and grass,
And meadowsweet, and haycocks dry,
No whit less still and lonely fair
Than the high cloudlets in the sky.

And for that minute a blackbird sang
Close by, and round him, mistier,
Farther and farther, all the birds
Of Oxfordshire and Gloucestershire.

Tall Nettles

Tall nettles cover up, as they have done
  These many springs, the rusty harrow, the plough
Long worn out, and the roller made of stone;
  Only the elm butt tops the nettles now.

This corner of the farmyard I like most:
  As well as any bloom upon a flower
I like the dust on the nettles, never lost
  Except to prove the sweetness of a shower.

Snow

In the gloom of whiteness,
In the great silence of snow,
A child was sighing
And bitterly saying: 'Oh,
They have killed a white bird up there on her nest,
The down is fluttering from her breast!'
And still it fell through the dusky brightness
On the child crying for the bird of the snow.

Digging

Today I think
Only with scents, – scents dead leaves yield,
And bracken, and wild carrot's seed,
And the square mustard field;

Odours that rise
When the spade wounds the root of tree,
Rose, currant, raspberry, or goutweed,
Rhubarb or celery;

The smoke's smell, too,
Flowing from where a bonfire burns
The dead, the waste, the dangerous,
And all to sweetness turns.

It is enough
To smell, to crumble the dark earth,
While the robin sings over again
Sad songs of Autumn mirth.

As the Team's Head-Brass

As the team's head-brass flashed out on the turn
The lovers disappeared into the wood.
I sat among the boughs of the fallen elm
That strewed the angle of the fallow, and
Watched the plough narrowing a yellow square
Of charlock. Every time the horses turned
Instead of treading me down, the ploughman leaned
Upon the handles to say or ask a word,
About the weather, next about the war.
Scraping the share he faced towards the wood,
And screwed along the furrow till the brass flashed
Once more.
    The blizzard felled the elm whose crest
I sat in, by a woodpecker's round hole,
The ploughman said. 'When will they take it away?'
'When the war's over.' So the talk began
One minute and an interval of ten,
A minute more and the same interval.
'Have you been out?' 'No.' 'And don't want to, perhaps?'
'If I could only come back again, I should.
I could spare an arm. I shouldn't want to lose
A leg. If I should lose my head, why, so,
I should want nothing more . . . Have many gone
From here?' 'Yes.' 'Many lost?' 'Yes, a good few.
Only two teams work on the farm this year.
One of my mates is dead. The second day
In France they killed him. It was back in March,
The very night of the blizzard, too. Now if

He had stayed here we should have moved the tree.'
'And I should not have sat here. Everything
Would have been different. For it would have been
Another world.' 'Aye, and a better, though
If we could see all all might seem good.' Then
The lovers came out of the wood again:
The horses started and for the last time
I watched the clods crumble and topple over
After the ploughshare and the stumbling team.

But These Things Also

But these things also are Spring's –
On banks by the roadside the grass
Long-dead that is greyer now
Than all the Winter it was;

The shell of a little snail bleached
In the grass; chip of flint, and mite
Of chalk; and the small birds' dung
In splashes of purest white:

All the white things a man mistakes
For earliest violets
Who seeks through Winter's ruins
Something to pay Winter's debts,

While the North blows, and starling flocks
By chattering on and on
Keep their spirits up in the mist,
And Spring's here, Winter's not gone.

Edward Thomas

The Owl

Downhill I came, hungry, and yet not starved;
Cold, yet had heat within me that was proof
Against the North wind; tired, yet so that rest
Had seemed the sweetest thing under a roof.

Then at the inn I had food, fire, and rest,
Knowing how hungry, cold, and tired was I.
All of the night was quite barred out except
An owl's cry, a most melancholy cry

Shaken out long and clear upon the hill,
No merry note, nor cause of merriment,
But one telling me plain what I escaped
And others could not, that night, as in I went.

And salted was my food, and my repose,
Salted and sobered, too, by the bird's voice
Speaking for all who lay under the stars,
Soldiers and poor, unable to rejoice.

Sue Cowling

Sue Cowling loves the seaside and always wanted to be a mermaid when she grew up. Every now and then she runs away to the seaside from her home in Birmingham, but her husband and grown-up daughter and son keep bringing her back. This may be because her cooking is generally reckoned to be good – however, she did once serve navy-blue pasta (after dyeing some shorts) to surprised guests. It tasted OK though. Originally from Merseyside, Sue is proud of the fact that she can spot a phoney Liverpool accent in ten seconds flat! Her nightmare would be getting stuck on a train without a book.

She finds that poems often arrive unexpectedly during the night. She scribbles them down in the dark on a notepad beside the bed, then next morning tries to work out what she has written! If it's a daytime poem the ideas are jotted down on her hand – they have been known to end up halfway up her arm! She's not sure why but her poems sometimes seem to have a mind of their own and take a bizarre turn when they're supposed to be serious or decide to rhyme when they've been told not to.

haiku

dawn is delicious
soup made from dew and birdsong
drink it with your ears

Hair Growing

Hair grows a centimetre a month
Or a third of a millimetre a day.
That means
That while you've been reading this poem
Your hair
(And mine)
Will have grown
A billimetre,
A trillimetre,
A zillimetre
Or a squillimetre!
It depends how fast you read.

Sue Cowling

Cleopatra

You
Sunbaked sleeper,
Belly-creeper,
High-heeled walker,
Stealthy stalker,
Four-foot faller,
Caterwauler,
Mobile mousetrap –
Close the cat flap!

Late-Night Caller

The tick of the clock,
the click of the lock,
a shoeless sock
on the stair,

the groan of the floor,
the squeak of a door,
the sigh of a drawer –
who's there?

A current of air,
a pencil of light –
'I'm back, son. All right?
Goodnight!'

Sue Cowling

The Elephant Child

Under an African sun he stands,
the elephant child,
hot and hungry and thirsty.
He's as big as a car
but still small for an elephant.
Sadly swinging his trunk he stands
for many hours beside his mother,
trying to coax and nudge her back to life
to take him home.
He could not help her when the men came.
They just laughed at him.
And now
under an African moon he stands
and tries to make sense of her butchered face.
Then he cries as only an elephant can cry
but he does not understand.
Neither do I.

Recipe for a Class Outing

Ingredients:
30 children, washed and scrubbed
29 packed lunches (no bottles)
3 teachers
an equal quantity of mums
1 nosebleed
2 fights
a hot day
3 lost purses
1 slightly torn dress
plenty of sweets
5 or 6 songs (optional)

Method:
Place children and adults in a bus and heat slowly.
Season well with sweets, reserving a few for later.
Heat to boiling point. Add fights and nosebleed.
Leave to simmer for 2 hours.
Remove children and packed lunches and leave to cool.
Stir in torn dress and lost purses.
Return to heat, add songs to taste.
Mix thoroughly. If the children go soggy and start to stick
together, remove from the bus and drain.
At the end of the cooking time divide into individual
portions (makes about 36).
Serve with relief, garnished liberally with dirt.

Sue Cowling

Leaves

My wellingtons swish
through the leaves.
I am four years old again, at play
in the crumpled wrapping paper
of the year.

Ogden Nash

Ogden Nash was born in New York. When he was seven years old, he developed a serious eye infection that meant he had to stay in bed in a darkened room for nearly a year. He was not permitted to use his eyes, so his mother read to him and took on his schooling. He went on to become the editor of Doubleday. He is most famous for his poetry, but he also was the lyricist for several musicals on Broadway. He wrote the lyrics for *One Touch of Venus* (with Kurt Weill), *He and She*, *Sweet Bye and Bye*, *Two's Company* and *The Littlest Review*. Smokey Robinson has even said that Nash is his favourite songwriter of all time.

Ogden Nash

The Octopus

Tell me, O Octopus, I begs,
Is those things arms, or is they legs?
I marvel at thee, Octopus;
If I were thou, I'd call me Us.

The Cow

The cow is of the bovine ilk;
One end is moo, the other, milk.

Good Riddance But Now What?

Come, children, gather round my knee;
Something is about to be.

Tonight's December thirty-first,
Something is about to burst.

The clock is crouching, dark and small,
Like a time bomb in the hall.

Hark! It's midnight, children dear.
Duck! Here comes another year.

The Wendigo

The Wendigo,
The Wendigo!
Its eyes are ice and indigo!
Its blood is rank and yellowish!
Its voice is hoarse and bellowish!
Its tentacles are slithery,
And scummy,
Slimy,
Leathery!
Its lips are hungry blubbery,
And smacky,
Sucky,
Rubbery!

The Wendigo,
The Wendigo!
I saw it just a friend ago!
Last night it lurked in Canada;
Tonight, on your veranada!
As you are lolling hammockwise
It contemplates you stomachwise.
You loll,
It contemplates,
It lollops.
The rest is merely gulps and gollops.

The Purist

I give you now Professor Twist,
A conscientious scientist,
Trustees exclaimed, 'He never bungles!'
And sent him off to distant jungles.
Camped on a tropic riverside,
One day he missed his loving bride.
She had, the guide informed him later,
Been eaten by an alligator.
Professor Twist could not but smile.
'You mean,' he said, 'a crocodile.'

Saturday

Fame Was a Claim of Uncle Ed's

Fame was a claim of Uncle Ed's,
Simply because he had three heads,
Which, if he'd only had a third of,
I think he would never have been heard of.

The Adventures of Isabel

Isabel met an enormous bear,
Isabel, Isabel, didn't care;
The bear was hungry, the bear was ravenous,
The bear's big mouth was cruel and cavernous.
The bear said, Isabel, glad to meet you,
How do, Isabel, now I'll eat you!
Isabel, Isabel, didn't worry,
Isabel didn't scream or scurry,
She washed her hands and she straightened her hair up,
Then Isabel quietly ate the bear up.

Once in a night as black as pitch
Isabel met a wicked witch.
The witch's face was cross and wrinkled,
The witch's gums with teeth were sprinkled.
Ho ho, Isabel! the old witch crowed,
I'll turn you into an ugly toad!
Isabel, Isabel, didn't worry,
Isabel didn't scream or scurry,
She showed no rage, she showed no rancor,
But she turned the witch into milk and drank her.

Isabel met a hideous giant,
Isabel continued self-reliant.
The giant was hairy, the giant was horrid,
He had one eye in the middle of his forehead.
Good morning, Isabel, the giant said,
I'll grind your bones to make my bread.
Isabel, Isabel, didn't worry,
Isabel didn't scream or scurry.
She nibbled the zwieback that she always fed off,
And when it was gone, she cut the giant's head off.

Isabel met a troublesome doctor,
He punched and he poked till he really shocked her.
The doctor's talk was of coughs and chills
And the doctor's satchel bulged with pills.
The doctor said unto Isabel,
Swallow this, it will make you well.
Isabel, Isabel, didn't worry,
Isabel didn't scream or scurry.
She took those pills from the pill concoctor,
And Isabel calmly cured the doctor.

Isabel once was asleep in bed
When a horrible dream crawled into her head.
It was worse than a dinosaur, worse than a shark,
Worse than an octopus oozing in the dark.
'Boo!' said the dream, with a dreadful grin,
'I'm going to scare you out of your skin!'
Isabel, Isabel, didn't worry,
Isabel didn't scream or scurry,
Isabel had a cleverer scheme;
She just woke up and fooled that dream.

Whenever you meet a bugaboo
Remember what Isabel used to do.
Don't scream when the bugaboo says 'Boo!'
Just look it in the eye and say, 'Boo to you!'
That's how to banish a bugaboo;
Isabel did it and so can you!
Boooooo to you.

Wilfred Owen

Wilfred Owen was born in Shrewsbury, and was already writing poetry and teaching in France when the First World War began. He enlisted in 1915 as he was horrified by the extent of the fighting, but by 1917 he was injured and sent back to the UK. It was in a war hospital that he met Siegfried Sassoon, who was also being treated for shellshock.

Sassoon was already a poet and he proved to be a mentor for Owen, looking at his poems and introducing him to other writers such as Robert Graves, Arnold Bennett and H. G. Wells. Owen returned to the front in August 1918, where he was awarded the Military Cross for bravery, but tragically, on 4 November 1918, just seven days before the end of the war, he was caught in a German machine-gun attack and killed. He was only twenty-five. The bells were ringing on 11 November 1918 to celebrate the Armistice when his parents received the telegram informing them of Wilfred's untimely death.

He is one of the most famous poets from the time of the First World War, writing poems such as 'Dulce Et Decorum Est' and 'Anthem for Doomed Youth'.

Strange Meeting

It seemed that out of battle I escaped
Down some profound dull tunnel, long since scooped
Through granites which titanic wars had groined.

Yet also there encumbered sleepers groaned,
Too fast in thought or death to be bestirred.
Then, as I probed them, one sprang up, and stared
With piteous recognition in fixed eyes,
Lifting distressful hands, as if to bless.
And by his smile, I knew that sullen hall,
By his dead smile I knew we stood in Hell.

With a thousand pains that vision's face was grained;
Yet no blood reached there from the upper ground,
And no guns thumped, or down the flues made moan.
'Strange friend,' I said, 'here is no cause to mourn.'
'None,' said that other, 'save the undone years,
The hopelessness. Whatever hope is yours,
Was my life also; I went hunting wild
After the wildest beauty in the world,
Which lies not calm in eyes, or braided hair,
But mocks the steady running of the hour,
And if it grieves, grieves richlier than here.
For by my glee might many men have laughed,
And of my weeping something had been left,
Which must die now. I mean the truth untold,
The pity of war, the pity war distilled.
Now men will go content with what we spoiled,

Or, discontent, boil bloody, and be spilled.
They will be swift with swiftness of the tigress.
None will break ranks, though nations trek from progress.
Courage was mine, and I had mystery,
Wisdom was mine, and I had mastery:
To miss the march of this retreating world
Into vain citadels that are not walled.
Then, when much blood had clogged their chariot-wheels,
I would go up and wash them from sweet wells,
Even with truths that lie too deep for taint.
I would have poured my spirit without stint
But not through wounds; not on the cess of war.
Foreheads of men have bled where no wounds were.

'I am the enemy you killed, my friend.
I knew you in this dark: for so you frowned
Yesterday through me as you jabbed and killed.
I parried; but my hands were loath and cold.
Let us sleep now . . .'

Greater Love

Red lips are not so red
As the stained stones kissed by the English dead.
Kindness of wooed and wooer
Seems shame to their love pure.
O Love, your eyes lose lure
When I behold eyes blinded in my stead!

Your slender attitude
Trembles not exquisite like limbs knife-skewed,
Rolling and rolling there
Where God seems not to care;
Till the fierce love they bear
Cramps them in death's extreme decrepitude.

Your voice sings not so soft,
Though even as wind murmuring through raftered loft,
Your dear voice is not dear,
Gentle, and evening clear,
As theirs whom none now hear,
Now earth has stopped their piteous mouths that coughed.

Heart, you were never hot
Nor large, nor full like hearts made great with shot;
And though your hand be pale,
Paler are all which trail
Your cross through flame and hail:
Weep, you may weep, for you may touch them not.

Anthem for Doomed Youth

What passing-bells for these who die as cattle?
Only the monstrous anger of the guns.
Only the stuttering rifles' rapid rattle
Can patter out their hasty orisons.
No mockeries now for them; no prayers nor bells;
Nor any voice of mourning save the choirs,
The shrill, demented choirs of wailing shells;
And bugles calling for them from sad shires.

What candles may be held to speed them all?
Not in the hands of boys but in their eyes
Shall shine the holy glimmers of good-byes.
The pallor of girls' brows shall be their pall;
Their flowers the tenderness of patient minds,
And each slow dusk a drawing-down of blinds.

Dulce Et Decorum Est

Bent double, like old beggars under sacks,
Knock-kneed, coughing like hags, we cursed through sludge,
Till on the haunting flares we turned our backs
And towards our distant rest began to trudge.
Men marched asleep. Many had lost their boots
But limped on, blood-shod. All went lame; all blind;
Drunk with fatigue; deaf even to the hoots
Of tired, outstripped Five-Nines that dropped behind.

Gas! Gas! Quick, boys! – An ecstasy of fumbling,
Fitting the clumsy helmets just in time;
But someone still was yelling out and stumbling
And flound'ring like a man in fire or lime . . .
Dim, through the misty panes and thick green light,
As under a green sea, I saw him drowning.

In all my dreams, before my helpless sight,
He plunges at me, guttering, choking, drowning.

If in some smothering dreams you too could pace
Behind the wagon that we flung him in,
And watch the white eyes writhing in his face,
His hanging face, like a devil's sick of sin;
If you could hear, at every jolt, the blood
Come gargling from the froth-corrupted lungs,
Obscene as cancer, bitter as the cud
Of vile, incurable sores on innocent tongues,
My friend, you would not tell with such high zest
To children ardent for some desperate glory,
The old Lie: Dulce et decorum est
Pro patria mori.

Futility

Move him into the sun
Gently its touch awoke him once,
At home, whispering of fields unsown.
Always it woke him, even in France,
Until this morning and this snow.
If anything might rouse him now
The kind old sun will know.

Think how it wakes the seeds
Woke once the clays of a cold star.
Are limbs, so dear-achieved, are sides
Full-nerved, still warm, too hard to stir?
Was it for this the clay grew tall?
O what made fatuous sunbeams toil
To break earth's sleep at all?

Spring Offensive

Halted against the shade of a last hill
They fed, and eased of pack-loads, were at ease;
And leaning on the nearest chest or knees,
Carelessly slept. But many there stood still
To face the stark, blank sky beyond the ridge,
Knowing their feet had come to the end of the world.
Marvelling they stood, and watched the long grass swirled
By the May breeze, murmurous with wasp and midge;
And though the summer oozed into their veins
Like an injected drug for their bodies' pains,
Sharp on their souls hung the imminent ridge of grass,
Fearfully flashed the sky's mysterious glass.

Hour after hour they ponder the warm field
And the far valley behind, where the buttercups
Had blessed with gold their slow boots coming up;
When even the little brambles would not yield
But clutched and clung to them like sorrowing arms.
They breathe like trees unstirred.

Till like a cold gust thrills the little word
At which each body and its soul begird
And tighten them for battle. No alarms
Of bugles, no high flags, no clamorous haste,
Only a lift and flare of eyes that faced
The sun, like a friend with whom their love is done.
O larger shone that smile against the sun,
Mightier than his whose bounty these have spurned.

So, soon they topped the hill, and raced together
Over an open stretch of herb and heather
Exposed. And instantly the whole sky burned
With fury against them; earth set sudden cups
In thousands for their blood; and the green slope
Chasmed and steepened sheer to infinite space.

Of them who running on that last high place
Breasted the surf of bullets, or went up
On the hot blast and fury of hell's upsurge,
Or plunged and fell away past this world's verge,
Some say God caught them even before they fell.

But what say such as from existence' brink
Ventured but drave too swift to sink,
The few who rushed in the body to enter hell,
And there out-fiending all its fiends and flames
With superhuman inhumanities,
Long-famous glories, immemorial shames
And crawling slowly back, have by degrees
Regained cool peaceful air in wonder
Why speak not they of comrades that went under?

The Send-Off

Down the close, darkening lanes they sang their way
To the siding-shed,
And lined the train with faces grimly gay.

Their breasts were stuck all white with wreath and spray
As men's are, dead.

Dull porters watched them, and a casual tramp
Stood staring hard,
Sorry to miss them from the upland camp.

Then, unmoved, signals nodded, and a lamp
Winked to the guard.

So secretly, like wrongs hushed-up, they went.
They were not ours:
We never heard to which front these were sent;

Nor there if they yet mock what women meant
Who gave them flowers.

Shall they return to beatings of great bells
In wild train-loads?
A few, a few, too few for drums and yells,

May creep back, silent, to village wells,
Up half-known roads.

Gina Douthwaite

Gina Douthwaite lives in a barn on the Yorkshire Wolds. It used to be full of corn and tractors and cows. Now it's full of books and computers and dogs. As a child she was animal-mad, preferring cats to dolls, collecting stray dogs and riding a one-eyed pony. School holidays were spent helping out at a vet's and later she trained in Animal Health, working with farm animals all over the country. She's well at home in a barn.

She began to write when her two daughters started school. Many of her poems are based on the things they said and did. That's why her first collection of shape poetry, *Picture a Poem*, is dedicated to them – the 'Sisters'. Her second collection, *What Shapes an Ape?*, stems from her love of animals and the opportunities she has to observe them out in the woods and fields which surround her home.

When not writing, reading or walking dogs, Gina enjoys running Shape Poetry workshops in schools and has, for many years, been a Creative Writing tutor conducting courses in venues as diverse as colleges to caves . . . but that's another story.

Captivating Creature

Elephant roaming in forest, on grassland,
using her trunk like a hand and an arm,
sucking up water to spray as a shower,
wafting palm ears when the sun gets too warm,
dusting herself with a trunkful of dry sand,
ripples of wrinkles encompassing eyes.
On thick pillar legs she's at peace with her power,
at ease with a brain hardly mammoth in size.

Captive Creature

Elephant restless in circus, in zoo,
pacing and pawing at concrete and bar,
longing for freedom and wide-open spaces,
leading processions, bedecked with *howdah*,
drooping with feathers and wearing a tutu,
learning, on two legs, to balance and dance.
Juggling with balls. Being put through such paces
doesn't give dignity much of a chance.

Gina Douthwaite

Night Mer

One night when I was fast apeels
all duggled snown and warm
I had a very dasty ream
about a stunder thorm
and fightning lashed
and saves at wea
like boiling werpents sithed
and foaming angs did frockle me
and shicked and slucked and eyethed.
They ulled me under, lungings full
of fevvered, fluffin fug
till suffing grably I apized
upon the redboom bug.

Dark Day

Lamp-posts stand like sparklers
spitting rays of light into the night,

blobs of yellow jellyfish
wriggle in pathway puddles.

Bullets of rain ricochet,
run rivers in sleeve creases,

make lakes across boxed lunches
of crushed crisps, sandwiches,

clutched by huddled children
on a dark day way to school.

River

Whispers round the roots of willows,
wallows well in rocky hollows,
washes white the wide-stride weirs,
wades to waterfalls and rears
its rumbling rage into a roar
of writhing ivory before
it runs away – waves farewell with a
wink of whirlpool. Wily river.

Hydropod Slob

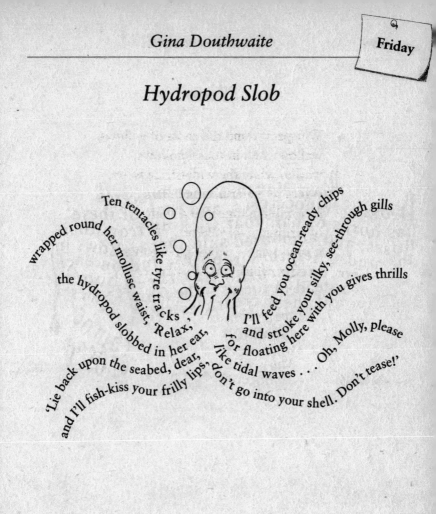

Ten tentacles like tyre tracks

wrapped round her mollusc waist,

the hydropod slobbed in her ear, 'Relax,

'Lie back upon the seabed, dear,

and I'll fish-kiss your frilly lips,

I'll feed you ocean-ready chips

and stroke your silky, see-through gills

for floating here with you gives thrills

like tidal waves . . . Oh, Molly, please

don't go into your shell. Don't tease!'

Gina Douthwaite

Rhino

When more than one rhinoceros
becomes rhinoceroses, and each of these
has horns of hair that stick up from their
noses, and armoured skin that wallows in
the mud when they reposes, and on each
foot each rhino has three hoofs
instead of toeses – the features
of these creatures show
the problem
language poses
when more
than one
rhinoceros

becomes
rhinoc-
eroses.

This Kissing Business

Should I part my lips, or pucker?
Bite them tightly? Blow or suck or

hold my breath? Perhaps I'll practise
on my mirror. See the fact is

I'm not sure what is expected
when four lips become connected.

Colin West

Colin West says: 'I grew up in the 1950s to the strains of *Davy, Davy Crockett, king of the wild frontier*, and *Robin Hood, Robin Hood, riding through the glen*. (If you want to know how the tunes go, just ask anyone over fifty!) First of all I wanted to be an artist, then an actor in Westerns, then a magician, then a songwriter, and finally an artist again! And I've always enjoyed making up funny rhymes, so when I started adding my own drawings to them, I realized the best job of all is that of poet/illustrator. It's wonderful making people laugh, and so I usually try to fill my work with as much humour as possible. But I also try to provide the occasional "quieter" piece, to give readers a break from non-stop laughter! My hobbies include music (especially musical shows with lots of dancing), looking at old things (buildings, ruins, antiques, etc.), collecting books (mainly poetry ones with good illustrations), and perhaps most of all, thinking up new stories and poems for children to enjoy.'

Joker

I am the Joker in the pack
The card who makes you smile.
I'm not like King or Queen or Jack,
I am the Joker in the pack –
The cheeky one who answers back
And tells you all the while:
'I am the Joker in the pack,
The card who makes you smile.'

Tuesday

Pogo Stick

Upon my pogo stick I pounce
And out of school I homeward bounce.
I bounce so high, how my heart pounds
Until at last I'm out of bounds.

Magic Me This

Magic me this,
and Magic me that,
a new bell and collar
for Kitty my cat.

Magic me that,
and Magic me this,
a frog who's awaiting
a princess to kiss.

Magic me this,
and Magic me that,
a new broom to fly on
at night like a bat.

Magic me that,
and Magic me this,
then long may I cackle
and Kitty may hiss.

This House

This house, now you're away,
Misses you more each day;
Its every little room
Has its own special gloom.
The handles on the doors
Wait for a touch that's yours;
The sofa and the chairs
Long for your seat on theirs.
This house with just me in it
Misses you more each minute.

My Colours

These are
My colours,
One by one:

Red –
The poppies
Where I run.

Orange –
Summer's
Setting sun.

Yellow –
Farmers'
Fields of corn.

Green –
The clover
On my lawn.

Blue –
The sea
Where fishes spawn.

Indigo –
A starling's
Feather.

Violet –
The dancing
Heather.

A rainbow
They make
All together.

Is Reading Aloud . . . ?

Is reading aloud
in this library allowed,
or is reading aloud
not allowed?

Well, reading aloud
is allowed in this library –

AS LONG AS IT
ISN'T TOO LOUD.

Some Stuff in a Sack

One summer's day at half past three
Old Ginger Tom went off to sea,
With some stuff in a sack,
And a parrot called Jack,
Sing Fiddle-dee-fiddle-dee-dee.

Beneath the sun he dozed a while,
Then woke up by a desert isle,
With some stuff in a sack,
Like two boots big and black,
And a parrot called Jack,
Sing Fiddle-dee-fiddle-dee-dee.

He crossed a jungle dark and dim
And nothing seemed to bother him,
With some stuff in a sack,
Like a drum he could whack,
And a parrot called Jack,
Sing Fiddle-dee-fiddle-dee-dee.

He gathered wood beside a lake
And built a fire and took a break,
With some stuff in a sack,
Like a fish finger snack,
And a parrot called Jack,
Sing Fiddle-dee-fiddle-dee-dee.

He met a fearsome pirate crew
But knew exactly what to do,
With some stuff in a sack,
Like a whip that went crack,
And a parrot called Jack,
Sing Fiddle-dee-fiddle-dee-dee.

And then he walked along the shore
And thought he'd put to sea once more,
With some stuff in a sack,
Like a map to get back,
And a parrot called Jack,
Sing Fiddle-dee-fiddle-dee-dee.

And when there came a mighty storm,
Old Ginger Tom slept snug and warm
With some stuff in a sack,
Like a waterproof mac,
And a parrot called Jack,
Sing Fiddle-dee-fiddle-dee-dee.

He woke up when the storm had passed
And saw that he was home at last,
With no stuff in the sack,
(Nothing left to unpack),
Sing Fiddle-dee-fiddle-dee-dee.

And all next day the tale he told
Of Tom's Adventures, Brave and Bold
With some stuff in a sack,
Like two boots big and black,
And a drum he could whack,
And a fish finger snack,
And a whip that went crack,
And a map to get back,
And a waterproof mac,
But that parrot called Jack
Sang: FIDDLE-DEE-FIDDLE-DEE-DEE!

John Hegley

John Hegley drew his first breath in London and went to school in Luton, where he liked to do rhymes and cartoons in the birthday cards he made for his dad. At the age of twelve he was very glad to be given a pair of glasses; he'd wanted some since he was five. Many years later he worked with two children's theatre companies, Soapbox and Professor Dogg's Troupe, before becoming the popular and highly original stand-up comedian, poet, singer, songwriter and glasses-wearer that he is today.

The emergensea

The octopus awoke one morning and wondered
  what rhyme it was.
Looking at his alarm-clocktopus
he saw that it had stopped
and it was time to stop having a rest
and get himself dressed.
On every octofoot
he put
an octosocktopus
but in his hurry, one foot got put
not into an octosocktopus
but into an electric plug socket
and the octopus got a nasty electric shocktopus
and had to call the octodoctopus
who couldn't get in
to give any help or medicine
because the door was loctopus.
The octopus couldn't move, being in a state of
  octoshocktopus
so the octodoctopus bashed the door
to the floor
and the cure was as simple as could be:
a nice refreshing cup of
seawater.

Uncle and Auntie

My auntie gives me a colouring book and crayons
I begin to colour
after a while auntie leans over and says
you've gone over the lines
what do you think they're for
eh?
some kind of statement is it?
going to be a rebel are we?
your auntie gives you a lovely present
and you have to go and ruin it
I begin to cry
my uncle gives me a hanky and some blank paper
do some doggies of your own he says
I begin to colour
when I have done
he looks over
and says they are all very good
he is lying
only some of them are

Limberick

There was once a woman of Gwent
who was useless at pitching a tent
she hammered a peg
through a bone in her leg
and immediately after, she went
aaaaaaaaaaaargh.

Red Poem

DANGER,
Don't tip that
strawberry jam
into the post-box
STOP, STOP! If the Post
Office van turns up now you'll be so
embarrassed,
Dad.

John Hegley

What a poem's not

A poem is not an Ant
but it can be quite short.
A poem is not a Banana
but there may be something under its skin.
A poem is not a Coat
but it may have some warmth in it.
A poem is not a Dog
and it can do without a basket.
A poem is not an Endless pair of trousers
but it can be quite long.
A poem is not a Football
shaped like a cucumber.
A poem is not a Goat shaped like
a piece of chewing-gum.
A poem is not a Hedgehog
but it might be hard to get hold of.
A poem is not an Idiot
but it can be quite stupid.
A poem is not a Jack-in-the-box
but it can be quite stupid.
A poem is not a Kite
but it might blow away.
A poem is not a Light bulb
but you can change it if you want to.
A poem is not a Monkey
but it can be quite human.
A poem is not a Nut
but you can give it to a monkey.

A poem is not a Ookookookookookook
ookookookooloombomanumakookoo.
A poem is not a Prison
and it shouldn't feel like one either.
A poem is not a Question
actually it is sometimes.
A poem is not a Radio
but you may have to tune in to it.
A poem is not a Scab
so don't pick it.
A poem is not a Toothbrush
so don't clean your teeth with it.
A poem is not a Umbrella
but it may give protection.
A poem is not a Verruca
and I'm glad.
A poem is not a Wig
but you can wear it if you want to.
A poem is not an X-ray
make no bones about it.
A poem is not a Year-old bag of vegetables
but it can smell quite strongly.
A poem is not a Zylophone
and it can spell words wrongly.

John Hegley

A three-legged friend

They have a three-legged dog
and they call him Clover
and sometimes he falls over
and if he'd have had four legs
maybe they'd have called him
Lucky.

For the soup

There once was an organic leek
that had managed to learn how to speak,
at the sight of a knife
it would fear for its life
and go eeeeeeeeeeeeeeeeeeeeeek!

Index of First Lines

Index of Poets

Acknowledgements

The compiler and publisher would like to thank the following for permission to use copyright material:

Agard, John, 'Secret', 'Poetry Jump Up', 'The Hurt Boy and the Birds' from *Get Back Pimple* published by Penguin, 'First Morning' from *Laughter is an Egg*, Penguin, 'Don't Call an Alligator Long-Mouth Till You Cross the River' from *Say it Again Gran*, Penguin. All poems published by permission of John Agard c/o the Caroline Sheldon Literary Agency; **Berry, James**, all poems by permission of the author; **Bevan, Clare**, all poems by permission of the author; **Bloom**, Valerie, 'How to Ask for a Hamster', 'Frost' from *The World is Sweet* published by Bloomsbury Children's Books (2000). All poems by permission of the author; **Carter, James**, 'Love You More', 'Take a Poem', 'Icy Morning Haiku', 'Inside', 'Talking Time' by permission of the author; 'Electric Guitars' and 'The Dark' first published in *Cars, Stars, Electric Guitars*, Walker Books (2002); **Cookson, Paul**, all poems first published by Macmillan Children's Books except for 'Let No One Steal Your Dreams' first published in *Let No One Steal Your Dreams*, A Twist In The Tale, 1994 and 'Father's Hands' first published in *Father's Hands*, Solway, 1998. All poems published by permission of the author; **Corbett, Pie**, all poems first published by Macmillan Children's Books except 'Five Ways of Looking at a Lemon' and 'The Entertainment of Small Things' first published in *How to Teach Poetry Writing at Key Stage 3* by Pie Corbett, David Fulton Publishers 2002. All poems by permission of the author. **Cowling, Sue**, 'Haiku', 'Cleopatra' by permission of the author, 'Hair Growing' first published in *Kersplosh, Kersplash, Kersplat!*, Oxford University Press (2001), 'Late-Night Caller', 'The Elephant Child', 'Recipe for a Class Outing', 'Leaves' first published in *What Is A Kumquat?*, Faber (1991); **Dean, Jan**, 'It's Not What I'm Used To', 'Sheep Look White Until it Snows', 'A mother's Confession', 'Banned', 'Colouring In' by permission of the author, 'Angels' first published in *Nearly 13*, Blackie (1994); **Dixon, Peter**, all poems by permission of the author; **Douthwaite, Gina**, all poems by permission of the author; **Duffy, Carol Ann**, 'Sharp Freckles' and 'Meeting Midnight' first published in *Meeting Midnight*, Faber and Faber; 'The Oldest Girl in the World' first published in *The Oldest Girl in the World*, Faber and Faber, and 'Teacher', 'Dimples', 'A Week as My Home Town' and 'The Giantess' first published in *The Good Child's Guide to Rock and Roll*, Faber and Faber. All poems published by permission of the author; **Edwards, Richard**, all poems by permission of the author; **Farjeon, Eleanor**, 'It Was Long Ago', 'The Night Will Never Stay', 'Argus and Ulysses', 'Henry VIII', 'A Morning Song', 'Cats' and 'Christmas Stocking' from *Blackbird has Spoken*, Macmillan Children's Books, by permission of David Higham Associates on behalf of the estate of the author; **Foster,**

539

Acknowledgements

John, 'Summer Storm', 'November', 'It Isn't Right to Fight', 'Spells' first published in *Standing on the Sidelines*, Oxford University Press (1995), 'Five O'Clock Friday' first published in *Five O'Clock Friday*, Oxford University Press (1997), 'Dad's Hiding in the Shed' first published in *Making Waves*, Oxford University Press (1997), 'Spring Snow' first published in *Climb Aboard the Poetry Plane*, Oxford University Press (2000); **Fusek Peters, Andrew**, 'Fire At Night' and 'The Teflon Terror' by permission of the author; 'E-pet-aph' first published in *Sadderday and Funday*, Hodder-Wayland (2001), 'Poem for the Verbally Confused', 'The Gold Leaf Gangster' and 'The Letter' first published in *Moon Is On The Microphone*, Sherborne (1997/2000); 'Rap Up My Lunch' first published in *Ready Steady Rap*, Oxford University Press (2001); **Harmer, David**, all poems by permission of the author; **Hegley, John**, 'The emergensea', 'Uncle and Auntie', 'Limberick', 'Red Poem', 'What poem's not', 'A three-legged friend' and 'For the soup', from *My Dog is a Carrot*, Walker Books by permission of Peters, Fraser and Dunlop on behalf of the author; **Henderson, Stewart**, 'I'm Sorry' by permission of the author, 'How Do You Fuss An Octopus', 'Emily Prays to Elephants', 'Always Making Things' first published in *All Things Weird and Wonderful*, Lion Children's Books (2003), 'Sounds', 'Secret Friend', 'Who Left Grandad at the Chipshop?' first published in *Who Left Grandad at the Chipshop?*, Lion Children's Books (2000); **Joseph, Jenny**, all poems by permission of the author; **Kay, Jackie**, 'Brendon Gallacher' and 'Sassenachs' first published in *Two's Company*, Puffin Books, 'Summer Romance', 'Black Ann' and 'The Hole Story' first published in *The Frog Who Dreamt She Was An Opera Singer*, Bloomsbury. All poems by permission of the author; **MacRae, Lindsay**, all poems by permission of the author; **Magee, Wes**, all poems by permission of the author; **McGough, Roger**, Roger McGough c/o Peters Fraser and Dunlop for 'The Men Who Steals Dreams' and 'The Midnight Skaters' first published in *Pillow Talk*, Viking, 'The Snowman' first published in *Sky in the Pie*, Viking, 'Everything Touches' first published in *Lucky*, Viking, 'What I Love About School', 'Joy at the Sound' and 'Give and Take' first published in *Good Enough to Eat*, Viking, 'Storm', from *After the Merrymaking*, Cape; **McMillan, Ian**, all poems by permission of the author; **Milligan, Spike**, 'Onamatapia', 'On the Ning nang Nong', 'The Land of Bumbley Boo', 'Sardines', 'Bump!', 'Rain', 'Contagion', from *The Essential Spike Milligan*, Fourth Estate, by permission of Spike Milligan Productions Ltd; **Moses, Brian**, all poems by permission of the author; **Nash, Ogden**, 'The Octopus', 'The Cow', 'Good Riddance But Now What?', 'The Wendingo', 'The Purist', 'Fame Was a Claim of Uncle Ed's', 'The Adventures of Isabel' from *Candy is Dandy: The Best of Ogden Nash. Copyright* © 1953 by Ogden Nash, renewed, by permission of Curtis Brown Ltd on behalf of the author and Andre Deutsch Ltd; **Nichols, Grace**, 'For Forest' from *Come On Into My Tropical Garden*, A&C Black, 'Morning', 'Give Yourself A Hug' from *Give Yourself A Hug*, A&C Black. All poems by permission of Grace Nichols c/o Curtis Brown Ltd; **Owen, Gareth**, all poems by

Acknowledgements

permission of the author; **Patten, Brian**, 'Rabbit's Spring' first published in *Thawing Frozen Frogs*, Puffin Books; 'Looking for Dad', 'Gust Becos I Cud Not Spel' and 'Squeezes' first published in *Gargling with Jelly*, Puffin Books; and 'Geography Lesson', 'The Day I Got My Finger Stuck Up My Nose' first published in *Juggling with Gerbils*, Puffin Books and 'The Small Dragon' first published in *Love Poems*, Flamingo Books. All poems by permission of the author; **Phinn, Gervase**, all poems by permission of the author; **Rice, John**, 'Castle to be Built in the Woods', 'A Minute to Midnight', 'Climbing the World' by permission of the author, 'Constant, Constant Little Light' first published in *The Upside Down Frown*, Wayland (1999), 'On Some Other Planet' first published in *Rockets and Quasars*, Aten Press (1984), 'Driving at Night with My Dad' first published in *Dark As A Midnight Dream*, Evans Brothers (2000), 'Low Owl' first published in *Bears Don't Like Bananas*, Simon & Schuster (1991); **Scannell, Vernon**, all poems by permission of the author; **Stevens, Roger**, all poems by permission of the author; **Toczek, Nick**, all poems by permission of the author; **Turner, Steve**, all poems by permission of the author; **West, Colin**, all poems by permission of the author.

Every effort has been made to trace the copyright holders but if any have been inadvertently overlooked the publishers will be pleased to make the necessary arrangement at the first opportunity.